C-648

THIS IS YOUR **PASSBOOK**® FOR ...

PERSONNEL ASSOCIATE

NLC®

NATIONAL LEARNING CORPORATION®
passbooks.com

COPYRIGHT NOTICE

Copyright © 2020 by

NLC®

National Learning Corporation

212 Michael Drive, Syosset, NY 11791
(516) 921-8888 • www.passbooks.com
E-mail: info@passbooks.com

PUBLISHED IN THE UNITED STATES OF AMERICA

PASSBOOK® SERIES

THE *PASSBOOK® SERIES* has been created to prepare applicants and candidates for the ultimate academic battlefield – the examination room.

At some time in our lives, each and every one of us may be required to take an examination – for validation, matriculation, admission, qualification, registration, certification, or licensure.

Based on the assumption that every applicant or candidate has met the basic formal educational standards, has taken the required number of courses, and read the necessary texts, the *PASSBOOK® SERIES* furnishes the one special preparation which may assure passing with confidence, instead of failing with insecurity. Examination questions – together with answers – are furnished as the basic vehicle for study so that the mysteries of the examination and its compounding difficulties may be eliminated or diminished by a sure method.

This book is meant to help you pass your examination provided that you qualify and are serious in your objective.

The entire field is reviewed through the huge store of content information which is succinctly presented through a provocative and challenging approach – the question-and-answer method.

A climate of success is established by furnishing the correct answers at the end of each test.

You soon learn to recognize types of questions, forms of questions, and patterns of questioning. You may even begin to anticipate expected outcomes.

You perceive that many questions are repeated or adapted so that you can gain acute insights, which may enable you to score many sure points.

You learn how to confront new questions, or types of questions, and to attack them confidently and work out the correct answers.

You note objectives and emphases, and recognize pitfalls and dangers, so that you may make positive educational adjustments.

Moreover, you are kept fully informed in relation to new concepts, methods, practices, and directions in the field.

You discover that you arre actually taking the examination all the time: you are preparing for the examination by "taking" an examination, not by reading extraneous and/or supererogatory textbooks.

In short, this PASSBOOK®, used directedly, should be an important factor in helping you to pass your test.

PERSONNEL ASSOCIATE

DISTINGUISHING FEATURES OF THE CLASS:
This position is responsible for assisting in providing administrative assistance and support in implementing personnel policies and procedures. The incumbent performs research, drafts reports and procedures, performs other assignments and special projects as directed. While the ability to exercise independent judgement and make independent decisions is required, general direction is received from administrative personnel. General supervision may be exercised over assigned personnel. Does related work as required.

TYPICAL WORK ACTIVITIES:
- Conducts research and drafts reports with recommendations on various personnel topics;
- Prepares drafts of policies and procedures and assists in the administration and communication of such policies and procedures;
- Conducts research in preparation for labor relations activities;
- Develops, conducts and analyzes survey results and response requests;
- Assists in the recruitment process;
- Conducts research on new or existing employee benefit programs and assists in the administration and communication of such programs;
- Assists in the development and presentation of training programs for employees;
- Confers with various departments, agencies and bureaus and evaluates and makes recommendations on various personnel matters;
- Responds to inquiries from departments, job applicants and the general public regarding human resource policies and procedures;
- Prioritizes work assignments and sets goals for the department;
- Assists with the administration of confidential and sensitive projects;
- Conducts studies and prepares reports and manuals regarding departmental operations, procedures and policies;
- Performs a variety of tasks involving the specialized work of the department.

SUBJECT OF EXAMINATION:
The written test is designed to evaluate knowledge, skills and/or abilities in the following areas:
1. **Preparing written material** - These questions test for the ability to present information clearly and accurately and to organize paragraphs logically and comprehensibly. For some questions, you will be given information in two or three sentences followed by four restatements of the information. You must then choose the best version. For other questions, you will be given paragraphs with their sentences out of order. You must then choose, from four suggestions and then asked to choose from four suggestions the best order for the sentences.
2. **Public personnel administration** - These questions test for knowledge of the principles and practices used in applying laws, rules, and policies to situations encountered in planning and executing the personnel functions in a government agency. Questions may cover such areas as recruitment, selection and placement; position classification; performance evaluation; and employee relations.

3. **Supervision** - These questions test for knowledge of the principles and practices employed in planning, organizing and controlling the activities of a work unit toward predetermined objectives. The concepts covered, usually in a situational question format, include such topics as assigning and reviewing work; evaluating performance; maintaining work standards; motivating and developing subordinates; implementing procedural change; increasing efficiency; and dealing with problems of absenteeism, morale and discipline.

4. **Understanding and interpreting written material** - These questions test for the ability to understand and interpret written material. You will be presented with brief reading passages and will be asked questions about the passage. You should base your answers to the questions only on what is presented in the passages and not on what you may happen to know about the topic.

HOW TO TAKE A TEST

I. YOU MUST PASS AN EXAMINATION

A. *WHAT EVERY CANDIDATE SHOULD KNOW*

Examination applicants often ask us for help in preparing for the written test. What can I study in advance? What kinds of questions will be asked? How will the test be given? How will the papers be graded?

As an applicant for a civil service examination, you may be wondering about some of these things. Our purpose here is to suggest effective methods of advance study and to describe civil service examinations.

Your chances for success on this examination can be increased if you know how to prepare. Those "pre-examination jitters" can be reduced if you know what to expect. You can even experience an adventure in good citizenship if you know why civil service exams are given.

B. *WHY ARE CIVIL SERVICE EXAMINATIONS GIVEN?*

Civil service examinations are important to you in two ways. As a citizen, you want public jobs filled by employees who know how to do their work. As a job seeker, you want a fair chance to compete for that job on an equal footing with other candidates. The best-known means of accomplishing this two-fold goal is the competitive examination.

Exams are widely publicized throughout the nation. They may be administered for jobs in federal, state, city, municipal, town or village governments or agencies.

Any citizen may apply, with some limitations, such as the age or residence of applicants. Your experience and education may be reviewed to see whether you meet the requirements for the particular examination. When these requirements exist, they are reasonable and applied consistently to all applicants. Thus, a competitive examination may cause you some uneasiness now, but it is your privilege and safeguard.

C. *HOW ARE CIVIL SERVICE EXAMS DEVELOPED?*

Examinations are carefully written by trained technicians who are specialists in the field known as "psychological measurement," in consultation with recognized authorities in the field of work that the test will cover. These experts recommend the subject matter areas or skills to be tested; only those knowledges or skills important to your success on the job are included. The most reliable books and source materials available are used as references. Together, the experts and technicians judge the difficulty level of the questions.

Test technicians know how to phrase questions so that the problem is clearly stated. Their ethics do not permit "trick" or "catch" questions. Questions may have been tried out on sample groups, or subjected to statistical analysis, to determine their usefulness.

Written tests are often used in combination with performance tests, ratings of training and experience, and oral interviews. All of these measures combine to form the best-known means of finding the right person for the right job.

II. HOW TO PASS THE WRITTEN TEST

A. NATURE OF THE EXAMINATION

To prepare intelligently for civil service examinations, you should know how they differ from school examinations you have taken. In school you were assigned certain definite pages to read or subjects to cover. The examination questions were quite detailed and usually emphasized memory. Civil service exams, on the other hand, try to discover your present ability to perform the duties of a position, plus your potentiality to learn these duties. In other words, a civil service exam attempts to predict how successful you will be. Questions cover such a broad area that they cannot be as minute and detailed as school exam questions.

In the public service similar kinds of work, or positions, are grouped together in one "class." This process is known as *position-classification*. All the positions in a class are paid according to the salary range for that class. One class title covers all of these positions, and they are all tested by the same examination.

B. FOUR BASIC STEPS

1) Study the announcement

How, then, can you know what subjects to study? Our best answer is: "Learn as much as possible about the class of positions for which you've applied." The exam will test the knowledge, skills and abilities needed to do the work.

Your most valuable source of information about the position you want is the official exam announcement. This announcement lists the training and experience qualifications. Check these standards and apply only if you come reasonably close to meeting them.

The brief description of the position in the examination announcement offers some clues to the subjects which will be tested. Think about the job itself. Review the duties in your mind. Can you perform them, or are there some in which you are rusty? Fill in the blank spots in your preparation.

Many jurisdictions preview the written test in the exam announcement by including a section called "Knowledge and Abilities Required," "Scope of the Examination," or some similar heading. Here you will find out specifically what fields will be tested.

2) Review your own background

Once you learn in general what the position is all about, and what you need to know to do the work, ask yourself which subjects you already know fairly well and which need improvement. You may wonder whether to concentrate on improving your strong areas or on building some background in your fields of weakness. When the announcement has specified "some knowledge" or "considerable knowledge," or has used adjectives like "beginning principles of..." or "advanced ... methods," you can get a clue as to the number and difficulty of questions to be asked in any given field. More questions, and hence broader coverage, would be included for those subjects which are more important in the work. Now weigh your strengths and weaknesses against the job requirements and prepare accordingly.

3) Determine the level of the position

Another way to tell how intensively you should prepare is to understand the level of the job for which you are applying. Is it the entering level? In other words, is this the position in which beginners in a field of work are hired? Or is it an intermediate or advanced level? Sometimes this is indicated by such words as "Junior" or "Senior" in the class title. Other jurisdictions use Roman numerals to designate the level – Clerk I, Clerk II, for example. The word "Supervisor" sometimes appears in the title. If the level is not indicated by the title, check the description of duties. Will you be working under very close supervision, or will you have responsibility for independent decisions in this work?

4) Choose appropriate study materials

Now that you know the subjects to be examined and the relative amount of each subject to be covered, you can choose suitable study materials. For beginning level jobs, or even advanced ones, if you have a pronounced weakness in some aspect of your training, read a modern, standard textbook in that field. Be sure it is up to date and has general coverage. Such books are normally available at your library, and the librarian will be glad to help you locate one. For entry-level positions, questions of appropriate difficulty are chosen – neither highly advanced questions, nor those too simple. Such questions require careful thought but not advanced training.

If the position for which you are applying is technical or advanced, you will read more advanced, specialized material. If you are already familiar with the basic principles of your field, elementary textbooks would waste your time. Concentrate on advanced textbooks and technical periodicals. Think through the concepts and review difficult problems in your field.

These are all general sources. You can get more ideas on your own initiative, following these leads. For example, training manuals and publications of the government agency which employs workers in your field can be useful, particularly for technical and professional positions. A letter or visit to the government department involved may result in more specific study suggestions, and certainly will provide you with a more definite idea of the exact nature of the position you are seeking.

III. KINDS OF TESTS

Tests are used for purposes other than measuring knowledge and ability to perform specified duties. For some positions, it is equally important to test ability to make adjustments to new situations or to profit from training. In others, basic mental abilities not dependent on information are essential. Questions which test these things may not appear as pertinent to the duties of the position as those which test for knowledge and information. Yet they are often highly important parts of a fair examination. For very general questions, it is almost impossible to help you direct your study efforts. What we can do is to point out some of the more common of these general abilities needed in public service positions and describe some typical questions.

1) General information

Broad, general information has been found useful for predicting job success in some kinds of work. This is tested in a variety of ways, from vocabulary lists to questions about current events. Basic background in some field of work, such as sociology or economics, may be sampled in a group of questions. Often these are principles which have become familiar to most persons through exposure rather than through formal training. It is difficult to advise you how to study for these questions; being alert to the world around you is our best suggestion.

2) Verbal ability

An example of an ability needed in many positions is verbal or language ability. Verbal ability is, in brief, the ability to use and understand words. Vocabulary and grammar tests are typical measures of this ability. Reading comprehension or paragraph interpretation questions are common in many kinds of civil service tests. You are given a paragraph of written material and asked to find its central meaning.

3) Numerical ability

Number skills can be tested by the familiar arithmetic problem, by checking paired lists of numbers to see which are alike and which are different, or by interpreting charts and graphs. In the latter test, a graph may be printed in the test booklet which you are asked to use as the basis for answering questions.

4) Observation

A popular test for law-enforcement positions is the observation test. A picture is shown to you for several minutes, then taken away. Questions about the picture test your ability to observe both details and larger elements.

5) Following directions

In many positions in the public service, the employee must be able to carry out written instructions dependably and accurately. You may be given a chart with several columns, each column listing a variety of information. The questions require you to carry out directions involving the information given in the chart.

6) Skills and aptitudes

Performance tests effectively measure some manual skills and aptitudes. When the skill is one in which you are trained, such as typing or shorthand, you can practice. These tests are often very much like those given in business school or high school courses. For many of the other skills and aptitudes, however, no short-time preparation can be made. Skills and abilities natural to you or that you have developed throughout your lifetime are being tested.

Many of the general questions just described provide all the data needed to answer the questions and ask you to use your reasoning ability to find the answers. Your best preparation for these tests, as well as for tests of facts and ideas, is to be at your physical and mental best. You, no doubt, have your own methods of getting into an exam-taking mood and keeping "in shape." The next section lists some ideas on this subject.

IV. KINDS OF QUESTIONS

Only rarely is the "essay" question, which you answer in narrative form, used in civil service tests. Civil service tests are usually of the short-answer type. Full instructions for answering these questions will be given to you at the examination. But in case this is your first experience with short-answer questions and separate answer sheets, here is what you need to know:

1) Multiple-choice Questions

Most popular of the short-answer questions is the "multiple choice" or "best answer" question. It can be used, for example, to test for factual knowledge, ability to solve problems or judgment in meeting situations found at work.

A multiple-choice question is normally one of three types—

- It can begin with an incomplete statement followed by several possible endings. You are to find the one ending which *best* completes the statement, although some of the others may not be entirely wrong.
- It can also be a complete statement in the form of a question which is answered by choosing one of the statements listed.
- It can be in the form of a problem – again you select the best answer.

Here is an example of a multiple-choice question with a discussion which should give you some clues as to the method for choosing the right answer:

When an employee has a complaint about his assignment, the action which will *best* help him overcome his difficulty is to
- A. discuss his difficulty with his coworkers
- B. take the problem to the head of the organization
- C. take the problem to the person who gave him the assignment
- D. say nothing to anyone about his complaint

In answering this question, you should study each of the choices to find which is best. Consider choice "A" – Certainly an employee may discuss his complaint with fellow employees, but no change or improvement can result, and the complaint remains unresolved. Choice "B" is a poor choice since the head of the organization probably does not know what assignment you have been given, and taking your problem to him is known as "going over the head" of the supervisor. The supervisor, or person who made the assignment, is the person who can clarify it or correct any injustice. Choice "C" is, therefore, correct. To say nothing, as in choice "D," is unwise. Supervisors have and interest in knowing the problems employees are facing, and the employee is seeking a solution to his problem.

2) True/False Questions

The "true/false" or "right/wrong" form of question is sometimes used. Here a complete statement is given. Your job is to decide whether the statement is right or wrong.

SAMPLE: A roaming cell-phone call to a nearby city costs less than a non-roaming call to a distant city.

This statement is wrong, or false, since roaming calls are more expensive.

This is not a complete list of all possible question forms, although most of the others are variations of these common types. You will always get complete directions for answering questions. Be sure you understand *how* to mark your answers – ask questions until you do.

V. RECORDING YOUR ANSWERS

Computer terminals are used more and more today for many different kinds of exams.

For an examination with very few applicants, you may be told to record your answers in the test booklet itself. Separate answer sheets are much more common. If this separate answer sheet is to be scored by machine – and this is often the case – it is highly important that you mark your answers correctly in order to get credit.

An electronic scoring machine is often used in civil service offices because of the speed with which papers can be scored. Machine-scored answer sheets must be marked with a pencil, which will be given to you. This pencil has a high graphite content which responds to the electronic scoring machine. As a matter of fact, stray dots may register as answers, so do not let your pencil rest on the answer sheet while you are pondering the correct answer. Also, if your pencil lead breaks or is otherwise defective, ask for another.

Since the answer sheet will be dropped in a slot in the scoring machine, be careful not to bend the corners or get the paper crumpled.

The answer sheet normally has five vertical columns of numbers, with 30 numbers to a column. These numbers correspond to the question numbers in your test booklet. After each number, going across the page are four or five pairs of dotted lines. These short dotted lines have small letters or numbers above them. The first two pairs may also have a "T" or "F" above the letters. This indicates that the first two pairs only are to be used if the questions are of the true-false type. If the questions are multiple choice, disregard the "T" and "F" and pay attention only to the small letters or numbers.

Answer your questions in the manner of the sample that follows:

32. The largest city in the United States is
   A. Washington, D.C.
   B. New York City
   C. Chicago
   D. Detroit
   E. San Francisco

1) Choose the answer you think is best. (New York City is the largest, so "B" is correct.)
2) Find the row of dotted lines numbered the same as the question you are answering. (Find row number 32)
3) Find the pair of dotted lines corresponding to the answer. (Find the pair of lines under the mark "B.")
4) Make a solid black mark between the dotted lines.

VI. BEFORE THE TEST

Common sense will help you find procedures to follow to get ready for an examination. Too many of us, however, overlook these sensible measures. Indeed, nervousness and fatigue have been found to be the most serious reasons why applicants fail to do their best on civil service tests. Here is a list of reminders:

- Begin your preparation early – Don't wait until the last minute to go scurrying around for books and materials or to find out what the position is all about.
- Prepare continuously – An hour a night for a week is better than an all-night cram session. This has been definitely established. What is more, a night a week for a month will return better dividends than crowding your study into a shorter period of time.
- Locate the place of the exam – You have been sent a notice telling you when and where to report for the examination. If the location is in a different town or otherwise unfamiliar to you, it would be well to inquire the best route and learn something about the building.
- Relax the night before the test – Allow your mind to rest. Do not study at all that night. Plan some mild recreation or diversion; then go to bed early and get a good night's sleep.
- Get up early enough to make a leisurely trip to the place for the test – This way unforeseen events, traffic snarls, unfamiliar buildings, etc. will not upset you.
- Dress comfortably – A written test is not a fashion show. You will be known by number and not by name, so wear something comfortable.
- Leave excess paraphernalia at home – Shopping bags and odd bundles will get in your way. You need bring only the items mentioned in the official notice you received; usually everything you need is provided. Do not bring reference books to the exam. They will only confuse those last minutes and be taken away from you when in the test room.
- Arrive somewhat ahead of time – If because of transportation schedules you must get there very early, bring a newspaper or magazine to take your mind off yourself while waiting.
- Locate the examination room – When you have found the proper room, you will be directed to the seat or part of the room where you will sit. Sometimes you are given a sheet of instructions to read while you are waiting. Do not fill out any forms until you are told to do so; just read them and be prepared.
- Relax and prepare to listen to the instructions
- If you have any physical problem that may keep you from doing your best, be sure to tell the test administrator. If you are sick or in poor health, you really cannot do your best on the exam. You can come back and take the test some other time.

VII. AT THE TEST

The day of the test is here and you have the test booklet in your hand. The temptation to get going is very strong. Caution! There is more to success than knowing the right answers. You must know how to identify your papers and understand variations in the type of short-answer question used in this particular examination. Follow these suggestions for maximum results from your efforts:

1) Cooperate with the monitor

The test administrator has a duty to create a situation in which you can be as much at ease as possible. He will give instructions, tell you when to begin, check to see that you are marking your answer sheet correctly, and so on. He is not there to guard you, although he will see that your competitors do not take unfair advantage. He wants to help you do your best.

2) Listen to all instructions

Don't jump the gun! Wait until you understand all directions. In most civil service tests you get more time than you need to answer the questions. So don't be in a hurry. Read each word of instructions until you clearly understand the meaning. Study the examples, listen to all announcements and follow directions. Ask questions if you do not understand what to do.

3) Identify your papers

Civil service exams are usually identified by number only. You will be assigned a number; you must not put your name on your test papers. Be sure to copy your number correctly. Since more than one exam may be given, copy your exact examination title.

4) Plan your time

Unless you are told that a test is a "speed" or "rate of work" test, speed itself is usually not important. Time enough to answer all the questions will be provided, but this does not mean that you have all day. An overall time limit has been set. Divide the total time (in minutes) by the number of questions to determine the approximate time you have for each question.

5) Do not linger over difficult questions

If you come across a difficult question, mark it with a paper clip (useful to have along) and come back to it when you have been through the booklet. One caution if you do this – be sure to skip a number on your answer sheet as well. Check often to be sure that you have not lost your place and that you are marking in the row numbered the same as the question you are answering.

6) Read the questions

Be sure you know what the question asks! Many capable people are unsuccessful because they failed to *read* the questions correctly.

7) Answer all questions

Unless you have been instructed that a penalty will be deducted for incorrect answers, it is better to guess than to omit a question.

8) Speed tests

It is often better NOT to guess on speed tests. It has been found that on timed tests people are tempted to spend the last few seconds before time is called in marking answers at random – without even reading them – in the hope of picking up a few extra points. To discourage this practice, the instructions may warn you that your score will be "corrected" for guessing. That is, a penalty will be applied. The incorrect answers will be deducted from the correct ones, or some other penalty formula will be used.

9) Review your answers

If you finish before time is called, go back to the questions you guessed or omitted to give them further thought. Review other answers if you have time.

10) Return your test materials

If you are ready to leave before others have finished or time is called, take ALL your materials to the monitor and leave quietly. Never take any test material with you. The monitor can discover whose papers are not complete, and taking a test booklet may be grounds for disqualification.

VIII. EXAMINATION TECHNIQUES

1) Read the general instructions carefully. These are usually printed on the first page of the exam booklet. As a rule, these instructions refer to the timing of the examination; the fact that you should not start work until the signal and must stop work at a signal, etc. If there are any *special* instructions, such as a choice of questions to be answered, make sure that you note this instruction carefully.

2) When you are ready to start work on the examination, that is as soon as the signal has been given, read the instructions to each question booklet, underline any key words or phrases, such as *least, best, outline, describe* and the like. In this way you will tend to answer as requested rather than discover on reviewing your paper that you *listed without describing*, that you selected the *worst* choice rather than the *best* choice, etc.

3) If the examination is of the objective or multiple-choice type – that is, each question will also give a series of possible answers: A, B, C or D, and you are called upon to select the best answer and write the letter next to that answer on your answer paper – it is advisable to start answering each question in turn. There may be anywhere from 50 to 100 such questions in the three or four hours allotted and you can see how much time would be taken if you read through all the questions before beginning to answer any. Furthermore, if you come across a question or group of questions which you know would be difficult to answer, it would undoubtedly affect your handling of all the other questions.

4) If the examination is of the essay type and contains but a few questions, it is a moot point as to whether you should read all the questions before starting to answer any one. Of course, if you are given a choice – say five out of seven and the like – then it is essential to read all the questions so you can eliminate the two that are most difficult. If, however, you are asked to answer all the questions, there may be danger in trying to answer the easiest one first because you may find that you will spend too much time on it. The best technique is to answer the first question, then proceed to the second, etc.

5) Time your answers. Before the exam begins, write down the time it started, then add the time allowed for the examination and write down the time it must be completed, then divide the time available somewhat as follows:

- If 3-1/2 hours are allowed, that would be 210 minutes. If you have 80 objective-type questions, that would be an average of 2-1/2 minutes per question. Allow yourself no more than 2 minutes per question, or a total of 160 minutes, which will permit about 50 minutes to review.
- If for the time allotment of 210 minutes there are 7 essay questions to answer, that would average about 30 minutes a question. Give yourself only 25 minutes per question so that you have about 35 minutes to review.

6) The most important instruction is to *read each question* and make sure you know what is wanted. The second most important instruction is to *time yourself properly* so that you answer every question. The third most important instruction is to *answer every question*. Guess if you have to but include something for each question. Remember that you will receive no credit for a blank and will probably receive some credit if you write something in answer to an essay question. If you guess a letter – say "B" for a multiple-choice question – you may have guessed right. If you leave a blank as an answer to a multiple-choice question, the examiners may respect your feelings but it will not add a point to your score. Some exams may penalize you for wrong answers, so in such cases *only*, you may not want to guess unless you have some basis for your answer.

7) Suggestions
   a. Objective-type questions
      1. Examine the question booklet for proper sequence of pages and questions
      2. Read all instructions carefully
      3. Skip any question which seems too difficult; return to it after all other questions have been answered
      4. Apportion your time properly; do not spend too much time on any single question or group of questions
      5. Note and underline key words – *all, most, fewest, least, best, worst, same, opposite,* etc.
      6. Pay particular attention to negatives
      7. Note unusual option, e.g., unduly long, short, complex, different or similar in content to the body of the question
      8. Observe the use of "hedging" words – *probably, may, most likely,* etc.
      9. Make sure that your answer is put next to the same number as the question
      10. Do not second-guess unless you have good reason to believe the second answer is definitely more correct
      11. Cross out original answer if you decide another answer is more accurate; do not erase until you are ready to hand your paper in
      12. Answer all questions; guess unless instructed otherwise
      13. Leave time for review

   b. Essay questions
      1. Read each question carefully
      2. Determine exactly what is wanted. Underline key words or phrases.
      3. Decide on outline or paragraph answer

4. Include many different points and elements unless asked to develop any one or two points or elements
5. Show impartiality by giving pros and cons unless directed to select one side only
6. Make and write down any assumptions you find necessary to answer the questions
7. Watch your English, grammar, punctuation and choice of words
8. Time your answers; don't crowd material

8) Answering the essay question

Most essay questions can be answered by framing the specific response around several key words or ideas. Here are a few such key words or ideas:

M's: manpower, materials, methods, money, management
P's: purpose, program, policy, plan, procedure, practice, problems, pitfalls, personnel, public relations
   a. Six basic steps in handling problems:
      1. Preliminary plan and background development
      2. Collect information, data and facts
      3. Analyze and interpret information, data and facts
      4. Analyze and develop solutions as well as make recommendations
      5. Prepare report and sell recommendations
      6. Install recommendations and follow up effectiveness

   b. Pitfalls to avoid
      1. *Taking things for granted* – A statement of the situation does not necessarily imply that each of the elements is necessarily true; for example, a complaint may be invalid and biased so that all that can be taken for granted is that a complaint has been registered
      2. *Considering only one side of a situation* – Wherever possible, indicate several alternatives and then point out the reasons you selected the best one
      3. *Failing to indicate follow up* – Whenever your answer indicates action on your part, make certain that you will take proper follow-up action to see how successful your recommendations, procedures or actions turn out to be
      4. *Taking too long in answering any single question* – Remember to time your answers properly

IX. AFTER THE TEST

Scoring procedures differ in detail among civil service jurisdictions although the general principles are the same. Whether the papers are hand-scored or graded by machine we have described, they are nearly always graded by number. That is, the person who marks the paper knows only the number – never the name – of the applicant. Not until all the papers have been graded will they be matched with names. If other tests, such as training and experience or oral interview ratings have been given, scores will be combined. Different parts of the examination usually have different weights. For example, the written test might count 60 percent of the final grade, and a rating of training and experience 40 percent. In many jurisdictions, veterans will have a certain number of points added to their grades.

After the final grade has been determined, the names are placed in grade order and an eligible list is established. There are various methods for resolving ties between those who get the same final grade – probably the most common is to place first the name of the person whose application was received first. Job offers are made from the eligible list in the order the names appear on it. You will be notified of your grade and your rank as soon as all these computations have been made. This will be done as rapidly as possible.

People who are found to meet the requirements in the announcement are called "eligibles." Their names are put on a list of eligible candidates. An eligible's chances of getting a job depend on how high he stands on this list and how fast agencies are filling jobs from the list.

When a job is to be filled from a list of eligibles, the agency asks for the names of people on the list of eligibles for that job. When the civil service commission receives this request, it sends to the agency the names of the three people highest on this list. Or, if the job to be filled has specialized requirements, the office sends the agency the names of the top three persons who meet these requirements from the general list.

The appointing officer makes a choice from among the three people whose names were sent to him. If the selected person accepts the appointment, the names of the others are put back on the list to be considered for future openings.

That is the rule in hiring from all kinds of eligible lists, whether they are for typist, carpenter, chemist, or something else. For every vacancy, the appointing officer has his choice of any one of the top three eligibles on the list. This explains why the person whose name is on top of the list sometimes does not get an appointment when some of the persons lower on the list do. If the appointing officer chooses the second or third eligible, the No. 1 eligible does not get a job at once, but stays on the list until he is appointed or the list is terminated.

X. HOW TO PASS THE INTERVIEW TEST

The examination for which you applied requires an oral interview test. You have already taken the written test and you are now being called for the interview test – the final part of the formal examination.

You may think that it is not possible to prepare for an interview test and that there are no procedures to follow during an interview. Our purpose is to point out some things you can do in advance that will help you and some good rules to follow and pitfalls to avoid while you are being interviewed.

What is an interview supposed to test?

The written examination is designed to test the technical knowledge and competence of the candidate; the oral is designed to evaluate intangible qualities, not readily measured otherwise, and to establish a list showing the relative fitness of each candidate – as measured against his competitors – for the position sought. Scoring is not on the basis of "right" and "wrong," but on a sliding scale of values ranging from "not passable" to "outstanding." As a matter of fact, it is possible to achieve a relatively low score without a single "incorrect" answer because of evident weakness in the qualities being measured.

Occasionally, an examination may consist entirely of an oral test – either an individual or a group oral. In such cases, information is sought concerning the technical knowledges and abilities of the candidate, since there has been no written examination for this purpose. More commonly, however, an oral test is used to supplement a written examination.

Who conducts interviews?

The composition of oral boards varies among different jurisdictions. In nearly all, a representative of the personnel department serves as chairman. One of the members of the board may be a representative of the department in which the candidate would work. In some cases, "outside experts" are used, and, frequently, a businessman or some other representative of the general public is asked to serve. Labor and management or other special groups may be represented. The aim is to secure the services of experts in the appropriate field.

However the board is composed, it is a good idea (and not at all improper or unethical) to ascertain in advance of the interview who the members are and what groups they represent. When you are introduced to them, you will have some idea of their backgrounds and interests, and at least you will not stutter and stammer over their names.

What should be done before the interview?

While knowledge about the board members is useful and takes some of the surprise element out of the interview, there is other preparation which is more substantive. It *is* possible to prepare for an oral interview – in several ways:

1) Keep a copy of your application and review it carefully before the interview

This may be the only document before the oral board, and the starting point of the interview. Know what education and experience you have listed there, and the sequence and dates of all of it. Sometimes the board will ask you to review the highlights of your experience for them; you should not have to hem and haw doing it.

2) Study the class specification and the examination announcement

Usually, the oral board has one or both of these to guide them. The qualities, characteristics or knowledges required by the position sought are stated in these documents. They offer valuable clues as to the nature of the oral interview. For example, if the job involves supervisory responsibilities, the announcement will usually indicate that knowledge of modern supervisory methods and the qualifications of the candidate as a supervisor will be tested. If so, you can expect such questions, frequently in the form of a hypothetical situation which you are expected to solve. NEVER go into an oral without knowledge of the duties and responsibilities of the job you seek.

3) Think through each qualification required

Try to visualize the kind of questions you would ask if you were a board member. How well could you answer them? Try especially to appraise your own knowledge and background in each area, *measured against the job sought*, and identify any areas in which you are weak. Be critical and realistic – do not flatter yourself.

4) Do some general reading in areas in which you feel you may be weak

For example, if the job involves supervision and your past experience has NOT, some general reading in supervisory methods and practices, particularly in the field of human relations, might be useful. Do NOT study agency procedures or detailed manuals. The oral board will be testing your understanding and capacity, not your memory.

5) Get a good night's sleep and watch your general health and mental attitude

You will want a clear head at the interview. Take care of a cold or any other minor ailment, and of course, no hangovers.

What should be done on the day of the interview?

Now comes the day of the interview itself. Give yourself plenty of time to get there. Plan to arrive somewhat ahead of the scheduled time, particularly if your appointment is in the fore part of the day. If a previous candidate fails to appear, the board might be ready for you a bit early. By early afternoon an oral board is almost invariably behind schedule if there are many candidates, and you may have to wait. Take along a book or magazine to read, or your application to review, but leave any extraneous material in the waiting room when you go in for your interview. In any event, relax and compose yourself.

The matter of dress is important. The board is forming impressions about you – from your experience, your manners, your attitude, and your appearance. Give your personal appearance careful attention. Dress your best, but not your flashiest. Choose conservative, appropriate clothing, and be sure it is immaculate. This is a business interview, and your appearance should indicate that you regard it as such. Besides, being well groomed and properly dressed will help boost your confidence.

Sooner or later, someone will call your name and escort you into the interview room. *This is it.* From here on you are on your own. It is too late for any more preparation. But remember, you asked for this opportunity to prove your fitness, and you are here because your request was granted.

What happens when you go in?

The usual sequence of events will be as follows: The clerk (who is often the board stenographer) will introduce you to the chairman of the oral board, who will introduce you to the other members of the board. Acknowledge the introductions before you sit down. Do not be surprised if you find a microphone facing you or a stenotypist sitting by. Oral interviews are usually recorded in the event of an appeal or other review.

Usually the chairman of the board will open the interview by reviewing the highlights of your education and work experience from your application – primarily for the benefit of the other members of the board, as well as to get the material into the record. Do not interrupt or comment unless there is an error or significant misinterpretation; if that is the case, do not hesitate. But do not quibble about insignificant matters. Also, he will usually ask you some question about your education, experience or your present job – partly to get you to start talking and to establish the interviewing "rapport." He may start the actual questioning, or turn it over to one of the other members. Frequently, each member undertakes the questioning on a particular area, one in which he is perhaps most competent, so you can expect each member to participate in the examination. Because time is limited, you may also expect some rather abrupt switches in the direction the questioning takes, so do not be upset by it. Normally, a board member will not pursue a single line of questioning unless he discovers a particular strength or weakness.

After each member has participated, the chairman will usually ask whether any member has any further questions, then will ask you if you have anything you wish to add. Unless you are expecting this question, it may floor you. Worse, it may start you off on an extended, extemporaneous speech. The board is not usually seeking more information. The question is principally to offer you a last opportunity to present further qualifications or to indicate that you have nothing to add. So, if you feel that a significant qualification or characteristic has been overlooked, it is proper to point it out in a sentence or so. Do not compliment the board on the thoroughness of their examination – they have been sketchy, and you know it. If you wish, merely say, "No thank you, I have nothing further to add." This is a point where you can "talk yourself out" of a good impression or fail to present an important bit of information. Remember, *you close the interview yourself.*

The chairman will then say, "That is all, Mr. _____, thank you." Do not be startled; the interview is over, and quicker than you think. Thank him, gather your belongings and take your leave. Save your sigh of relief for the other side of the door.

How to put your best foot forward
Throughout this entire process, you may feel that the board individually and collectively is trying to pierce your defenses, seek out your hidden weaknesses and embarrass and confuse you. Actually, this is not true. They are obliged to make an appraisal of your qualifications for the job you are seeking, and they want to see you in your best light. Remember, they must interview all candidates and a non-cooperative candidate may become a failure in spite of their best efforts to bring out his qualifications. Here are 15 suggestions that will help you:

1) Be natural – Keep your attitude confident, not cocky
If you are not confident that you can do the job, do not expect the board to be. Do not apologize for your weaknesses, try to bring out your strong points. The board is interested in a positive, not negative, presentation. Cockiness will antagonize any board member and make him wonder if you are covering up a weakness by a false show of strength.

2) Get comfortable, but don't lounge or sprawl
Sit erectly but not stiffly. A careless posture may lead the board to conclude that you are careless in other things, or at least that you are not impressed by the importance of the occasion. Either conclusion is natural, even if incorrect. Do not fuss with your clothing, a pencil or an ashtray. Your hands may occasionally be useful to emphasize a point; do not let them become a point of distraction.

3) Do not wisecrack or make small talk
This is a serious situation, and your attitude should show that you consider it as such. Further, the time of the board is limited – they do not want to waste it, and neither should you.

4) Do not exaggerate your experience or abilities
In the first place, from information in the application or other interviews and sources, the board may know more about you than you think. Secondly, you probably will not get away with it. An experienced board is rather adept at spotting such a situation, so do not take the chance.

5) If you know a board member, do not make a point of it, yet do not hide it

Certainly you are not fooling him, and probably not the other members of the board. Do not try to take advantage of your acquaintanceship – it will probably do you little good.

6) Do not dominate the interview

Let the board do that. They will give you the clues – do not assume that you have to do all the talking. Realize that the board has a number of questions to ask you, and do not try to take up all the interview time by showing off your extensive knowledge of the answer to the first one.

7) Be attentive

You only have 20 minutes or so, and you should keep your attention at its sharpest throughout. When a member is addressing a problem or question to you, give him your undivided attention. Address your reply principally to him, but do not exclude the other board members.

8) Do not interrupt

A board member may be stating a problem for you to analyze. He will ask you a question when the time comes. Let him state the problem, and wait for the question.

9) Make sure you understand the question

Do not try to answer until you are sure what the question is. If it is not clear, restate it in your own words or ask the board member to clarify it for you. However, do not haggle about minor elements.

10) Reply promptly but not hastily

A common entry on oral board rating sheets is "candidate responded readily," or "candidate hesitated in replies." Respond as promptly and quickly as you can, but do not jump to a hasty, ill-considered answer.

11) Do not be peremptory in your answers

A brief answer is proper – but do not fire your answer back. That is a losing game from your point of view. The board member can probably ask questions much faster than you can answer them.

12) Do not try to create the answer you think the board member wants

He is interested in what kind of mind you have and how it works – not in playing games. Furthermore, he can usually spot this practice and will actually grade you down on it.

13) Do not switch sides in your reply merely to agree with a board member

Frequently, a member will take a contrary position merely to draw you out and to see if you are willing and able to defend your point of view. Do not start a debate, yet do not surrender a good position. If a position is worth taking, it is worth defending.

14) Do not be afraid to admit an error in judgment if you are shown to be wrong

The board knows that you are forced to reply without any opportunity for careful consideration. Your answer may be demonstrably wrong. If so, admit it and get on with the interview.

15) Do not dwell at length on your present job

The opening question may relate to your present assignment. Answer the question but do not go into an extended discussion. You are being examined for a *new* job, not your present one. As a matter of fact, try to phrase ALL your answers in terms of the job for which you are being examined.

Basis of Rating

Probably you will forget most of these "do's" and "don'ts" when you walk into the oral interview room. Even remembering them all will not ensure you a passing grade. Perhaps you did not have the qualifications in the first place. But remembering them will help you to put your best foot forward, without treading on the toes of the board members.

Rumor and popular opinion to the contrary notwithstanding, an oral board wants you to make the best appearance possible. They know you are under pressure – but they also want to see how you respond to it as a guide to what your reaction would be under the pressures of the job you seek. They will be influenced by the degree of poise you display, the personal traits you show and the manner in which you respond.

ABOUT THIS BOOK

This book contains tests divided into Examination Sections. Go through each test, answering every question in the margin. At the end of each test look at the answer key and check your answers. On the ones you got wrong, look at the right answer choice and learn. Do not fill in the answers first. Do not memorize the questions and answers, but understand the answer and principles involved. On your test, the questions will likely be different from the samples. Questions are changed and new ones added. If you understand these past questions you should have success with any changes that arise. Tests may consist of several types of questions. We have additional books on each subject should more study be advisable or necessary for you. Finally, the more you study, the better prepared you will be. This book is intended to be the last thing you study before you walk into the examination room. Prior study of relevant texts is also recommended. NLC publishes some of these in our Fundamental Series. Knowledge and good sense are important factors in passing your exam. Good luck also helps. So now study this Passbook, absorb the material contained within and take that knowledge into the examination. Then do your best to pass that exam.

———

EXAMINATION SECTION

EXAMINATION SECTION
TEST 1

DIRECTIONS: Each question or incomplete statement is followed by several suggested answers or completions. Select the one that BEST answers the question or completes the statement. *PRINT THE LETTER OF THE CORRECT ANSWER IN THE SPACE AT THE RIGHT.*

1. The Public Services Careers Program is a manpower program

    A. designed to develop permanent employment opportunities for the disadvantaged
    B. designed to encourage college graduates to enter the field of public administration
    C. run by the federal government for private organizations
    D. designed to prepare physically handicapped persons for new positions

1.____

2. The Intergovernmental Personnel Act (P.L. 91-648) provides federal assistance to state and local governments for improving and strengthening personnel administration.
The one of the following which is NOT provided for in this Act is

    A. creation of a new personnel system for upper-level personnel
    B. expanded training programs
    C. improved personnel management
    D. interchange of employees between federal government and state and local governments

2.____

3. Kepner–Tregoc management training courses are MOST closely involved with

    A. management by objectives
    B. development of overall leadership qualities
    C. leadership style
    D. problem-solving techniques

3.____

4. The BASIC purpose of the Managerial Grid for training program is to train managers to

    A. have concern for both production and the people who produce
    B. utilize scientific problem-solving techniques
    C. maximize efficient communication
    D. improve the quality of their leadership in *brainstorming* sessions

4.____

5. In establishing employee development objectives, management must make sure that they are

    A. stated in broad terms
    B. relevant to job performance
    C. developed by a training expert
    D. written in the vocabulary of the training field

5.____

6. In order that group conferences serve their purpose of developing professional staff, it is essential that

    A. discussion of controversial matters be limited
    B. notes be taken by the participants
    C. participants be encouraged to take part in the discussions
    D. chairmanships be rotated at the meetings

6.____

7. A personnel officer receives a request to conduct a course for interested employees who   7.____
    have filed for a promotion examination. The request that the course be given on agency
    time is turned down.
    This action is

    A. *justified;* such courses do not contain content that serve to improve employee per-
        formance
    B. *justified;* the course is designed to benefit the individual primarily, not the agency
    C. *unjustified;* regardless of objective, any training related to City operations will have
        an affect on employee performance tangibly or intangibly
    D. *unjustified;* if productivity has been based on full use of employee time, productivity
        will suffer if time is allocated for such a course

8. Of the following, the PRIMARY objective of sensitivity training is to   8.____

    A. teach management principles to participants
    B. improve and refine the decision-making process
    C. give the participants insight as to how they are perceived by others
    D. improve the emotional stability of the participants

9. In considering the functions of a manager, it is clear that the FIRST step in building a   9.____
    quality work force is the manager's need to

    A. design jobs to meet the realities of the labor market
    B. examine the qualification requirements for his positions and eliminate those which
        appear to be controversial
    C. determine the methods to be used in reaching that special public deemed most
        suitable for the agency
    D. establish controls so that there is reasonable assurance that the plans established
        to staff the agency will be properly consummated

10. Based on data documenting the differences between healthy and unhealthy organiza-   10.____
    tions, which statement describes a healthy, as contrasted with an unhealthy, organiza-
    tion?

    A. Innovation is not widespread but exists in the hands of a few.
    B. Risks are not avoided but accepted as a condition of change.
    C. Decision-making is not dispersed but delegated to organizational levels.
    D. Conflict is not overt but resolved without confrontation.

11. Which of the following management actions is NOT conducive to greater job satisfaction?   11.____

    A. Diversifying tasks in the unit as much as feasible
    B. Permitting workers to follow through on tasks rather than carry out single segments
        of the process
    C. Avoiding the use of *project teams* or *task forces*
    D. Delegating authority to each layer of the hierarchy to the maximum extent possible

12. When the span of control of a manager or administrator is widened or increased, a MOST likely result is   12.____

    A. greater specificity of operational procedures
    B. a decrease in total worker–administrator contacts
    C. a blurring of objectives and goals
    D. an increase in responsibility of subordinates

13. Although *superagencies* may have value in assisting the chief executive to supervise operations more efficiently, a MAJOR shortcoming is that they   13.____

    A. may not provide more effective delivery of services to the public
    B. may limit the chief executive in his ability to find out what is happening within the agencies
    C. tend to reduce the responsibility of component agency heads for their own operations
    D. add costs that have little relation to the efforts to achieve administrative effectiveness

14. Business and psychological literature on managerial effectiveness is based for the MOST part on   14.____

    A. job analyses or descriptions about the management process
    B. field studies or observations about the outcome of effective management
    C. personal experiences or opinions about the traits good managers possess
    D. attitudes or perceptions of managers about organizational goals and strategies

15. The impression MOST likely to be gained from published surveys of traits necessary for management is that the lists   15.____

    A. limit identified traits to obvious human virtues
    B. lack precision in pinpointing behavioral elements
    C. emphasize negative rather than positive variables
    D. exclude attitudinal and motivational factors

16. Management concepts in public and private organizations have been undergoing drastic shifts as a consequence of a new view emerging from the recent synthesis of learning in the sciences. While still in its infancy, this development has challenged much of what has been considered accepted management theory for a long time.
This change is frequently referred to in current management literature as   16.____

    A. systems thinking   B. scientific management
    C. behavioral science   D. multivariate analysis

17. Assuming more and more importance every day, the subject of management has under-   17._____
gone prodigious change in recent times.
With respect to this development, the MOST valid expression concerning the current
status of management would be:

   A. Authoritative texts have progressed to the point where differences in the formal
treatment of the process of management are comparatively rare
   B. The generalized theory of management which has been synthesized recently by
scholars in the field has given the term *management* a fixed meaning and definition
from which revolutionary progress may now be anticipated
   C. Unity of conception, thought, and view about the process of management is still a
long way off
   D. Unity of conception, thought, and view about the process of management has
been achieved in administrative circles under the revolutionary concepts brought
into being as a result of the latest developments in computer technology

18. That there is no average man, the manager would be first to acknowledge. Yet the exi-   18._____
gencies of organized enterprise require that the assumption be made.
Of the following, the procedure or process that is PRIMARILY based on this assumption is the

   A. administration of discipline
   B. establishment of rules and regulations
   C. policy of job enlargement
   D. promotion policy

19. There are four or more phases in the process of manpower planning.   19._____
Of the following, the one which should be scheduled FIRST is

   A. gathering and analyzing data through manpower inventories and forecasts
   B. establishing objectives and policies through personnel and budget control units
   C. designing plan and action programs
   D. establishing production goals for the agency

20. When ranked in order of frequency of performance, studies show which of the following   20._____
ranks LOWEST among the functions performed by central personnel offices in local governments?

   A. Planning, conducting, and coordinating training
   B. Certifying or auditing payrolls
   C. Conducting personnel investigations
   D. Engaging in collective bargaining

21. Which of the following activities of an agency personnel division can BEST be consid-   21._____
ered a control function?

   A. Scheduling safety meetings for supervisory staff
   B. Consultation on a disciplinary problem
   C. Reminders to line units to submit personnel evaluations
   D. Processing requests for merit increases

22. Which of the following interview styles is MOST appropriate for use in a problem-solving situation?

    22.____

    A. Directed   B. Non-directive
    C. Stress   D. Authoritarian

23. Which of the following is a COMMONLY used measure of morale in an organization?

    23.____

    A. Turnover rate
    B. Espirit de corps
    C. Specialized division of labor
    D. Job satisfaction

24. According to studies in personnel and industrial psychology, information that travels along the *grapevine* or informal communication system in an organization usually follows a pattern BEST classified as

    24.____

    A. cluster—key informants tell several individuals, one of whom passes it on in the same way
    B. wheel—around through successive informants until it reaches the source
    C. chain—double informants linked to successive pairs
    D. random probability—informant tells anyone he happens to encounter, and so forth

25. A carefully devised program has been developed in a certain city for combining performance evaluation and seniority into a formula to determine order of layoff. The essence of this plan is first to group employees of a particular job class into *seniority blocks* and then to use performance evaluation as a basis for determining layoff order within each seniority block.
The BEST of the following inferences which can be made from the above paragraph is that

    25.____

    A. this plan is unfair since seniority is not given sufficient weight in the selection process
    B. this city is probably behind most civil service jurisdictions in the evaluation of employee performance
    C. combining performance and seniority cannot be done since it is like *combining apples and oranges*
    D. under this plan, it is conceivable that a person with high seniority could be laid off before a person with lower seniority

26. With any decentralization of personnel functions, specific procedures and rules are developed to assure conformance with relevant provisions of the Civil Service Law and the Rules and Regulations of the central personnel agency.
To the extent that these procedures are specific and detailed,

    26.____

    A. agency involvement in the execution of the decentralized function will be limited
    B. agency discretion in the administration of the decentralized function will be limited
    C. size and composition of agency personnel staff will tend to become fixed
    D. flexibility of application to bolster agency performance will be provided

27. While decentralization of personnel functions to give operating agencies more authority in personnel matters relating to their operations has been a goal of personnel policy, recentralization is an ever-present possibility. Of the following, the factor which is the BEST indicator of the desirability of recentralization is that

    A. inconsistent policies or inconsistent application of policies resulted when decentralized operations were instituted
    B. costs in terms of personnel and procedures increased significantly when decentralization was introduced
    C. the decentralization did not serve any real identifiable need
    D. agency personnel units were not prepared to handle the responsibilities delegated to them

27.____

28. Although the Department of Personnel has developed and maintains an Executive Roster, its use by agency heads to fill managerial positions has been disappointing.
Of the following, the one that is the LEAST likely reason for NOT using the roster is that

    A. personal factors essential to the relationship of manager and administrator are not revealed in the roster record
    B. most agencies prefer to advance their own employees rather than use a general roster
    C. some agency heads think of experienced City managerial employees as superannuated administrative deadwood
    D. use of the roster implies a reduction of the scope of administrative discretion in selection

28.____

29. During one program year, an examiner found a number of occasions in which a special task, a special report, or some activity outside of planned programs had to be assigned. One staff member continually offered to undertake these assignments whenever the administrative examiner requested a volunteer. He handled these jobs in timely fashion even though he had begun the year with a full-time workload.
Of the following, the conclusion MOST warranted from the information given is that the

    A. staff member was much more efficient than other examiners in the division in planning and executing work
    B. staff member's regular workload actually was less than a full-time assignment for him
    C. commitment and will to serve was greater in this member than in others
    D. quality of work of other examiners may have been higher than that of this staff member

29.____

30. An examiner has three subordinate supervisors, each responsible for a major program in his division. He finds that one supervisor is much weaker than the other two, both in his planning of work and in his follow-through to achieve timely completion of tasks. To bolster the *weak* supervisor, the administrative examiner reassigns his best examiners to this unit.
This decision is POOR primarily because

    A. the performance of the competent examiners is likely to suffer eventually
    B. the assigned examiners will be expected to make more decisions themselves
    C. the ineffective supervisor might have done better by assignment elsewhere
    D. indicated disciplinary action was not taken

30.____

31. Because of the frustrations felt by many public administrators who have been unable to motivate their subordinates, the classic civil service reform movement has been condemned by observers of the public government scene. Those condemning that movement believe that the system has failed to develop a quality public service precisely because of the policies implemented as a result of the reform movement.
They suggest that the remedy lies in

    31.____

    A. centralizing the personnel functions in the hands of an elite group of professional personnel practitioners who would be best equipped to initiate needed remedies
    B. changing the concept of personnel management to a generalist approach, thus guaranteeing a broader and more integrated resolution of employee problems
    C. finding and implementing more practical personnel techniques in dealing with the various functional personnel areas
    D. completely decentralizing personnel administration to the responsible agency heads

32. The British scholar and statesman Harold J. Laski has stated that the expert was too likely to *make his subject the measure of life, instead of making life the measure of his subject.*
When applying this comment to the modern public service administrator, it is meant that the administrator should

    32.____

    A. expand the jurisdiction of his authority so that better integration among functional areas is possible
    B. personally be receptive to the concept of change and not merely concerned with protecting the methods of the past
    C. develop a group of specialists in functional subject matter areas in order to give better service to the operating department heads
    D. see the relationship of his own particular area of jurisdiction to other governmental activities and to the private sector

33. Suppose that, as an examiner, you are asked to prepare a budget for the next fiscal year for a division performing personnel functions.
Of the following, the consideration which is LEAST important to your development of the division budget involves

    33.____

    A. adequacy of the current year's budget for your division
    B. changes in workload that can be anticipated
    C. budget restrictions that have been indicated in a memorandum covering budget preparation
    D. staff reassignments which are expected during that fiscal year

34. Suppose you have been designated chairman of an intra-departmental committee to implement a major policy decision. The one of the following which is LEAST desirable as a subject for a planning meeting is   34.____

    A. determination of details of execution by each bureau
    B. specific allocation of responsibility for the phases of administration
    C. provision of means for coordination and follow-up
    D. formulation of sub-goals for each bureau

35. Collective bargaining challenges the concept of the neutrality of the personnel function in the public service. Which one of the following statements BEST reflects this observation?   35.____

    A. Personnel offices must clearly serve as a bridge between management and employees.
    B. In most cases, negotiation involves a tripartite group—labor relations, fiscal or budget, and the employee organization.
    C. Personnel bureaus must be identified openly with the public employer.
    D. Personnel units cannot make policy or commitments in labor relations; their primary function is to execute personnel decisions made by others.

36. Changes in the field of public employee labor relations have been both numerous and significant in recent years. Below are four statements that an examiner preparing a report on developments in this area of personnel management might possibly include as correct: 36.____

    I. At least one-third of the states give some type of bargaining rights to their employees
    II. Less than half the states have granted public employees the right to organize
    III. Since 1959, at least eight states have enacted comprehensive labor relations laws affecting public employees
    IV. By 1966, state and local governments had entered into more than 1,000 separate agreements with employee organizations

Which of the following choices lists the statements that are CORRECT?

    A. I, II, and III are correct, but not IV
    B. I, III, and IV are correct, but not II
    C. I and III are correct, but not II and IV
    D. II and III are correct, but not I and IV

37. Which of the following is NOT a major goal of unions in contract negotiations?   37.____

    A. Establishing management prerogatives
    B. Preserving and strengthening the union
    C. Promoting social and economic objectives
    D. Promoting the status of the union representatives

Questions 38–39.

DIRECTIONS: Answer Questions 38 and 39 on the basis of the following paragraph.

*An impending reorganization within an agency will mean loss by transfer of several pro-
fessional staff members from the personnel division. The division chief is asked to designate
the persons to be transferred. After reviewing the implications of this reduction of staff with his
assistant, the division chief discussed the matter at a staff meeting. He adopts the recommendations of several staff members to have volunteers make up the required reduction.*

38.   The decision to permit personnel to volunteer for transfer is   38._____

    A.   *poor;* it is not likely that the members of a division are of equal value to the division
       chief
    B.   *good;* dissatisfied members will probably be more productive elsewhere
    C.   *poor;* the division chief has abdicated his responsibility to carry out the order given
       to him
    D.   *good;* morale among remaining staff is likely to improve in a more cohesive frame-
       work

39.   Suppose one of the volunteers is a recently appointed employee who has completed his   39._____
probationary period acceptably, but whose attitude toward division operations and
agency administration tends to be rather negative and sometimes even abrasive.
Because of his lack of commitment to the division, his transfer is recommended.
If the transfer is approved, the division chief should, prior to the transfer,

    A.   discuss with the staff the importance of commitment to the work of the agency and
       its relationship with job satisfaction
    B.   refrain from any discussion of attitude with the employee
    C.   discuss with the employee his concern about the employee's attitude
    D.   avoid mention of attitude in the evaluation appraisal prepared for the receiving divi-
       sion chief

40.   It is time to make position classification a real help to line officials in defining programs   40._____
and objectives and structuring tasks to meet those objectives, rather than continuing to
act as a post auditor and controller.
Of the following, the statement which BEST reflects the sense of this passage is that

    A.   post audit and control procedures should be related to the prior processes of
       objectives and goals determination
    B.   position classification should be part of management decisions rather than an eval-
       uation of them
    C.   program definition requires prior determination of position characteristics and per-
       formance factors to facilitate management program decisions
    D.   primary responsibility for position classification and grade or level allocation is that
       of line management, not that of the classification specialist

41. Pencil and paper objective testing procedures have tremendous advantages of quantifi-
cation and empiricism. They are economical in production and use. But the procedures
have a great disadvantage in that they are designed primarily for statistical prediction.
A conclusion that is MOST consistent with the above statement is that

    A. statistical prediction becomes meaningless if the applicants tested constitute a
stratified sample and not a representative sample of the population
    B. predictions of adequate performance by any one group of successful applicants
will follow the normal curve
    C. if the group is small, statistical indices cannot have high validity
    D. such test procedures cannot predict the job success or failure of a specific appli-
cant

41._____

42. It has been stated that in the public service, the use of written tests is more appropriate
for selecting from among those outside the organization than from those within the organization.
This is so since

    A. written tests serve to reduce the number of final competitors to manageable pro-
portions
    B. vouchering of prospective employees from outside the organization is deemed to
be invalid and not reliable
    C. written tests are in effect substitutes for direct observation on the gob
    D. testing outside applicants for aptitude and achievement has served a useful pur-
pose in the elimination of extraneous prejudicial factors in the selection process

42._____

43. The *Test Validation Board* is a recent innovation.
The MAJOR purpose of this board is to review

    A. and approve questions to be used before the written test is held
    B. and approve the test questions and the proposed key answers immediately after
the test is held
    C. the test items and protests and then establish the final key answers
    D. the test items and protests and then recommend adoption of a final rating key

43._____

44. *Brainstorming* sessions include each of the following EXCEPT

    A. free-wheeling or wild ideas
    B. criticism of any idea
    C. great quantities of ideas
    D. combining or building on ideas

44._____

45. It has been ascertained that a certain top-level position should NOT be placed in the
competitive class.
What determines whether the new position should be placed in the non–competitive
class rather than in the exempt class?

    A. Subordinate positions are in the competitive class.
    B. An executive in a specific field is needed.
    C. The position can be subjected to examination.
    D. The position is policy making.

45._____

46. Personnel practice in most governmental organizations provides that a new employee   46.____
must serve a probationary period generally not to exceed six months. During this period,
he is to be given special attention in such matters as instruction, indoctrination, and general adjustment to his job. The theory behind this practice is that this period is the last
phase of the testing process, but the consensus is that the probationary period is not living up to its possibilities as a testing opportunity.
The MAJOR reason for this opinion is that the

    A. techniques used by personnel practitioners to encourage supervisors to pass
       objective judgments on probationers are not effective
    B. probationary period is too short and marginal employees can maintain their best
       behavior for this length of time
    C. supervisors are not living up to their obligation to conduct vigorous probationary
       appraisals
    D. supervisors try to avoid making unpleasant personal judgments about their
       employees

47. Plans were recently announced to require one year of college for entrance into the police   47.____
service and eventually a college degree for promotion in the police force.
Of the following, the one that will NOT present problems in implementing these plans is

    A. changing the Civil Service requirements for entrance or promotion
    B. overcoming police union objections to the promotion requirements
    C. providing sufficient time for affected individuals to meet these educational require-
       ments
    D. retaining college graduates in the police service over a period of years

Questions 48–50.

DIRECTIONS: Answer Questions 48 through 50 on the basis of the following paragraph.

*The increase in the extent to which each individual is personally responsible to others is
most noticeable in a large bureaucracy. No one person decides anything; each decision of
any importance is the product of an intricate process of brokerage involving individuals inside
and outside the organization who feel some reason to be affected by the decision, or who
have special knowledge to contribute to it. The more varied the organization's constituency,
the more outside "veto-groups" will need to be taken into account. But even if no outside con-
sultations were involved, sheer size would produce a complex process of decision. For a
large organization is a deliberately created system of tensions into which each individual is
expected to bring work–ways, viewpoints, and outside relationships markedly different from
those of his colleagues. It is the administrator's task to draw from these disparate forces the
elements of wise action from day to day, consistent with the purposes of the organization as a
whole.*

48. This passage is ESSENTIALLY a description of decision-making as   48.____

    A. an organization process
    B. the key responsibility of the administrator
    C. the one best position among many
    D. a complex of individual decisions

49. Which one of the following statements BEST describes the responsibilities of an adminis-   49.____
trator?
He

    A. modifies decisions and goals in accordance with pressures from within and outside the organization
    B. creates problem-solving mechanisms that rely on the varied interests of his staff and *veto-groups*
    C. makes determinations that will lead to attainment of his agency's objectives
    D. obtains agreement among varying viewpoints and interests

50. In the context of the operations of a central public personnel agency, a *veto-group* would   50.____
LEAST likely consist of

    A. employee organizations
    B. professional personnel societies
    C. using agencies
    D. civil service newspapers

KEY (CORRECT ANSWERS)

1. A	11. C	21. C	31. D	41. D
2. A	12. D	22. B	32. D	42. C
3. D	13. A	23. A	33. D	43. D
4. A	14. C	24. A	34. A	44. B
5. B	15. B	25. D	35. C	45. B
6. C	16. A	26. B	36. B	46. C
7. B	17. C	27. C	37. A	47. C
8. C	18. B	28. D	38. A	48. A
9. A	19. A	29. B	39. C	49. C
10. B	20. D	30. A	40. B	50. B

TEST 2

DIRECTIONS: Each question or incomplete statement is followed by several suggested answers or completions. Select the one that BEST answers the question or completes the statement. *PRINT THE LETTER OF THE CORRECT ANSWER IN THE SPACE AT THE RIGHT.*

1. The definition of merit system as it pertains to the public service is that a person's worth to the organization is the factor governing both his entrance and upward mobility within that service. The main ingredient used to accomplish entrance and mobility has been competition based on relative qualifications of candidates.
The burgeoning demands of new occupations and critical social and economic urgencies in the public service make it imperative that now

    1.____

   A. greater emphasis be placed on the intellectual and technical capacities of applicants in order to improve the high standards achieved by some professionals
   B. current methods be strengthened in order to make them more valid and reliable indicators among applicants for government positions
   C. public personnel officials work more closely with representatives of the various professions and occupations to establish more equitable minimum standards in order to improve the quality of its practitioners
   D. the system adapt to the new changes by establishing alternative methods more suitable to current needs

2. Civil service systems need to be reexamined from time to time to determine whether they are correctly fulfilling stated merit obligations. Frequently, inspection determines that what was once a valid practice ... has ceased to be an effective instrument and has become, instead, an unrealistic barrier to the implementation of merit principles. Which one of the following practices would be considered to be such an unrealistic barrier?

    2.____

   A. Disqualifying candidates with poor work history for positions involving the operation of trains or buses
   B. Disqualifying candidates for police work who have records of serious arrests
   C. Requiring a degree or license for medical, scientific, and professional positions
   D. Requiring a high school diploma for custodial, maintenance, and service positions

3. It is generally accepted that work attitudes and interpersonal relationships contribute at least as much as knowledge and ability to job performance. Several personality measuring and appraisal devices have been found useful in predicting personality and work attitudes.
A MAJOR drawback in their use in competitive selection, however, is the

    3.____

   A. *fakeability* of responses possible in such selection situations
   B. cost of the materials and their interpretation
   C. inability of these measures to predict actual job performance
   D. lack of reviewability of these devices

4. Human Relations School discoveries having a major impact on modern personnel prac-   4.____
   tices include all of the following EXCEPT that

   A. social as well as physical capacity determines the amount of work an employee
      does
   B. non-economic rewards play a central role in employee motivation
   C. the higher the degree of specialization, the more efficient the division of labor
   D. workers react to management as members of groups rather than as individuals

5. Studies of the relationship between creativity and intelligence indicate that creativity   5.____

   A. is one of several special intelligence factors
   B. consists primarily of general intelligence as measured by standardized tests
   C. involves non-intellective factors as well as minimums of intelligence
   D. relates more directly to quantitative than to verbal aptitudes and skills

6. Strategies of data collection applicable to personnel work can be grouped into two broad   6.____
   categories: the mechanical method in which data be collected according to pre-estab-
   lished guidelines, rules, or procedures, and the clinical method in which the manner of
   data collection may differ from candidate to candidate at the discretion of the professional person collecting it.
   An argument that has proved VALID in support of the clinical method is that

   A. no sound basis exists for writing any single set of rules for collecting data
   B. no known mechanical procedure can fully anticipate all potentially relevant data
   C. mechanical processes stress the use of techniques such as synthetic validation
   D. mechanical methods are inadequate for formulating optimal individualized predic-
      tion rules

7. Which one of the following actions appears LEAST mandated by the Griggs vs. Duke   7.____
   Power Company decision of the U.S. Supreme Court on discriminatory employment
   practice?

   A. Study of certification and appointment policies and procedures
   B. Determination of job performance standards as related to successful performance
   C. Review of personal history forms, applications, and interviews involved in employ-
      ment procedures
   D. Test validation by correlation of individual test items with total test scores

8. In decision-making terminology, the type of action taken on a problem when the deci-   8.____
   sion–maker finds that he cannot do anything to eliminate the cause is MOST often called
   _____ action.

   A. corrective   B. adaptive
   C. stopgap   D. interim

9. The Intergovernmental Personnel Act became law recently. This Act does NOT provide for   9._____

    A. temporary assignment of personnel between governmental jurisdiction
    B. grants for improving personnel administration and training
    C. interstate compacts for personnel and training activities
    D. a National Advisory Council to study federal personnel administration and make recommendations to the President and Congress

10. Following are three kinds of performance tests for which arrangements might be made to give the candidates a pretest warm-up period: 10._____
     I. typing
     II. truck driving
     III. stenography
Which one of the following choices lists all of the above tests that should be preceded by a warm-up session?

    A. I, III   B. II *only*
    C. I, II, III   D. None of the above

Questions 11–12.

DIRECTIONS: Answer Questions 11 and 12 on the basis of the following paragraph.

Your role as human resources utilization experts is to submit your techniques to operating administrators, for the program must in reality be theirs, not yours. We in personnel have been guilty of encouraging operating executives to believe that these important matters affecting their employees are personnel department matters, not management matters. We should hardly be surprised, as a consequence, to find these executives playing down the role of personnel and finding personnel "routines" a nuisance, for these are not in the mainstream of managing the enterprise—or so we have encouraged them to believe.

11. The BEST of the following interpretations of the above paragraph is that   11._____

    A. personnel people have been guilty of *passing the buck* on personnel functions
    B. operating officials have difficulty understanding personnel techniques
    C. personnel employees have tended to usurp some functions rightfully belonging to management
    D. matters affecting employees should be handled by the personnel department

12. The BEST of the following interpretations of the above paragraph is that   12._____

    A. personnel departments have aided and abetted the formulation of negative attitudes on the part of management
    B. personnel people are labor relations experts and should carry out these duties
    C. personnel activities are not really the responsibility of management
    D. management is now being encouraged by personnel experts to assume some responsibility for personnel functions

13. Employee training can be described BEST as a process that 　　　　13.____

    A. increases retention of skills
    B. changes employees' knowledge, skills, or aptitudes
    C. improves the work methods used
    D. improves the work environment

14. With respect to the use of on-the-job training methods, the theory is that it is possible to 　　14.____
create maximally favorable conditions for learning while on the job. In actual practice, it
has been found that these favorable conditions are difficult to achieve.
The MAIN reason militating against such ideal conditions is that

    A. the primary function on the job is production, and training must, therefore, take
       second place
    B. an adequate number of skilled and knowledgeable employees is usually not avail-
       able to engage in effective person-to-person training
    C. expensive equipment and work space are tied up during training, which is not
       advantageous to establishing good rapport between trainer and trainee
    D. an appraisal of trainee learning under pressure of job demands is not conducive to
       showing the trainee the reasons for his mistakes

15. In most major studies directed toward identification of productive scientific personnel, the 　　15.____
MOST effective predictor has been

    A. biographical information
    B. motivational analysis
    C. tests of ideational flexibility
    D. high-level reasoning tests

16. Because interviewing is a difficult art, MOST personnel people who conduct interviews 　　16.____

    A. break the interview into specific units with pauses in between
    B. remain fairly constant in the technique they use despite differences of purpose and
       persons interviewed
    C. utilize non-directive techniques during their first few years of interviewing
    D. vary their style and technique in accordance with the purpose of the interview and
       the personality of the persons interviewed

17. When using the *in-basket* technique, it is NOT possible to obtain measures of the 　　17.____

    A. amount of work done in a given time
    B. extent to which the candidate seeks guidance before making decisions
    C. proportion of decisions that lead to actual cost savings
    D. proportion of work time devoted to prepatory activities

18. The MOST appropriate people to develop the definition for specific classes of positions in 　　18.____
order that they may serve as useful criteria for allocating positions to classes are the

    A. personnel experts in the area of job evaluation
    B. program practitioners
    C. job analysts working within other occupations under study
    D. organization and methods analysts

19. By its very nature and in order to operate effectively, a job classification system which groups jobs into broad occupational categories and then subdivides them into levels of difficulty and responsibility requires

    A. the upgrading of positions in order to raise the pay rates of incumbents
    B. a process in which lengthy job descriptions covering the allocation criteria are pre-requisites
    C. a certain amount of central control
    D. the transfer of classification authority from an *inside-track priesthood to* the operating official

19.____

20. A plan of classifying positions based on duties and responsibilities is not the same thing as a pay plan. Although the classification arrangement may be a vital element upon which a compensation structure is based and administered, there are differences between the two plans. The MAJOR distinction between these plans can be illustrated best by the fact that

    A. a uniform accounting system requires a uniform job terminology, which can be accomplished best by a classification plan
    B. the compensation plan can be changed without affecting the classification plan, and classes of positions can be rearranged on a pay schedule without changing the schedule
    C. job evaluation results in a common understanding of the job for which a rate is being set and for job-to-job comparison
    D. the classification principle of *equal pay for equal work* was instrumental in evolving pay reform

20.____

21. By stretching higher grade duties over as many jobs as possible, the position classifier makes for

    A. economy
    B. more effective performance
    C. effective use of the labor market
    D. higher operational costs

21.____

22. Contemporary information about what people want that is pertinent to potential entrants to the public service labor market indicates that a MAJOR want is

    A. more time for play and less time for work
    B. more personal privacy and fewer creature comforts
    C. more employee relationships and less organizational hierarchy
    D. more political participation and less partisan neutrality

22.____

23. An occupational rather than an organizational commitment to personnel administration as a professional field is MOST likely to prevail among personnel workers who perceive their work as part of a function that is

    A. designed to serve the employees of their agency
    B. dominated by necessary but uninteresting tasks
    C. dedicated to obtaining compliance with the law
    D. devoted to the human problems of organizations

23.____

24. The FIRST major strike by city employees which tested the Condon-Wadlin Act was by employees of the 24.____

    A. Sanitation Department   B. Police Department
    C. Fire Department   D. Department of Welfare

25. In the aftermath of the city transit strike of 1966, study groups were appointed to recommend ways in which such strikes could be avoided. 25.____
The recommendations made at that time by the Governor's Committee and the American Arbitration Association were especially significant in that they both

    A. included machinery for the settlement of labor disputes which was to be set up outside the regular civil service establishment
    B. advocated the retention of the legal prohibition against strikes by public employees
    C. agreed to imposition of heavy fines on the union in case of a strike
    D. opted for repeal of the section in the Condon-Wadlin Act which prohibited strikes

26. Of the following, which country was the pioneer in employee-management relationships within the public service? 26.____

    A. Canada   B. France   C. Australia   D. Mexico

27. There are notable similarities and differences between collective bargaining in industry and government. 27.____
In which of the following areas are the similarities GREATEST?

    A. Negotiable subjects   B. Bargaining processes
    C. Mediation and arbitration   D. Strikes

28. Traditionally, white-collar and professional workers resisted unionization both in government and in industry. This attitude has changed drastically among these workers since the late 1950's, however, particularly among public employees. 28.____
The BASIC cause behind this change among public employees was that

    A. organized labor trained its big union recruitment guns on organizing these workers in the face of the dwindling proportion of blue-collar people in the labor force
    B. these employees generally identified with middle-class America, which had now become union-oriented
    C. they felt deep frustration with the authoritarianism of public administrators who believed that the *merit system* process gave the employee all the protection he needed
    D. the continual upward spiral of inflation resulted in making these workers among those deemed economically disadvantaged and necessitated their joining in unions for their own protection

29. Union efforts to improve retirement benefits for public employees have caused concern in
the State legislature. Recently, a special legislative committee was ordered to determine
whether retirement benefits should remain a subject for collective bargaining or whether
they should be regulated by

    A. a bipartisan pension commission
    B. a board designated by management and labor
    C. large commercial insurance carriers
    D. the State Insurance Fund

29.____

30. The performance of personnel functions which are part of a comprehensive and inte-
grated program of personnel management is conditioned significantly by personnel policies. Which one of the following is the LEAST valid criterion of what positive policies can
accomplish?

    A. Functions are governed by rules which permit their being performed in line with the
desired goals of the organization.
    B. Guidance for executives restrains them from mishandling the specified functions
with which they have been entrusted.
    C. Standard decisions make it unnecessary for subordinates to ask their supervisors
how given problems should be handled.
    D. Goals are enunciated for the purpose of selecting candidates best equipped to
prove successful in the particular organizational milieu.

30.____

31. The GREATEST handicap of personnel systems which are predicated on the *corps of
people* concept rather than on job analysis is lack of facility for

    A. conducting program evaluation studies
    B. developing sound programs for the direction and control of productivity
    C. manpower planning
    D. determining the limits of authority and responsibility among managerial personnel

31.____

32. It is an anomaly that one of the greatest threats to maintaining classification plans ade-
quately is slowness in adjusting salaries to keep up with the changing labor market.
Thus, distortions of many classification plans occur.
This is MAINLY due to

    A. pressure from management officials to upgrade employees who have not received
salary range increases
    B. inability to maintain an adequate file of pertinent pay data
    C. conflict in the pay philosophy between maintaining external alignment and compa-
rability with union rates
    D. difficulty in distinguishing between the pay program and the fringe benefit package

32.____

19

33. A personnel agency charged with identifying candidates with the kind of creative talent that can be used in an organizational setting should look for a high degree of certain attributes among the candidate population. Below are listed four characteristics which may qualify as desirable attributes for the purpose indicated:
    I. Self-confidence
    II. Social conformity
    III. Mobility aspirations
    IV. Job involvement
Which of the following choices lists ALL of the above attributes which the personnel agency should look for?

  A. I, II, IV
  C. II, III, IV
  B. I, III, IV
  D. III, IV

34. With regard to educational standards for selection purposes, the U.S. Supreme Court has held that such requirements should be

  A. eliminated in most cases
  B. related to job success
  C. maintained whenever possible
  D. reduced as far as possible

35. In surveying job series which would be most conducive to job restructuring, most attention has focused on P, T, and M positions.
The benefits claimed for job restructuring include all of the following EXCEPT

  A. creating more interesting and challenging P, T, and M jobs
  B. increasing promotional opportunities for P, T, and M employees
  C. providing more job opportunities for the lesser skilled
  D. creating new promotional opportunities for those in low-skill or dead-end jobs

36. We must restructure as many job series as possible to allow entry into the service and to permit successful job performance without previous training and experience. In the type of restructuring alluded to, it is ESSENTIAL that

  A. job duties be rearranged to form a learning progression as well as a means of reaching work objectives
  B. educational achievement be minimized as a factor in determining progression to higher position rank
  C. separate and distinctive job series be created independent of existing job series
  D. lateral entry opportunities be emphasized

37. From the standpoint of equal opportunity, the MOST critical item operating personnel must focus on is

  A. hiring more minority applicants for top-level positions
  B. helping existing minority employees upgrade their skills so they may qualify for higher skilled positions
  C. placing minority candidates in job categories where, there is little minority representation
  D. eliminating merit system principles

20

38. Most of the jobs opened up in human services through new career development efforts have been filled by women.
Of the following, the MAIN reason for this result is that the

    A. need to develop suitable careers for women is the major focus of the program
    B. majority of new career jobs are in fields where the work normally has been done by women
    C. labor shortages are found in fields that draw heavily on womanpower
    D. legislation and funds provide guides which emphasize the employment of women who are disadvantaged or underemployed

38.____

39. Thirty years ago, the Federal District Court granted a preliminary injunction restraining the city school system's board of examiners from conducting supervisory examinations or issuing lists based on them.
The reason given for this judicial action was that the

    A. disadvantaged and minority group members were given preferential treatment
    B. eligibility requirements were too high
    C. rating used was based on a *pass–fail* scoring system
    D. tests discriminated against Blacks and Puerto Ricans

39.____

40. The city recently began making thousands of jobs available to the unemployed and underemployed. This program, administered by the Human Resources Administration, implements the Federal Emergency Employment Act.
The federal statute provides that FIRST priority for such jobs be given to

    A. heads of households
    B. persons living alone
    C. veterans of the Indochina or Korean War
    D. youths entering the labor market

40.____

41. According to the Equal Employment Opportunity Act of 1966, a covered employer may NOT

    A. discriminate against an individual because he is a member of the Communist Party in the United States
    B. indicate preference for or limitation to national origin in printing a notice or advertisement for employment
    C. employ only members of a certain religion if the employer is an educational institution owned or supported by that religion
    D. apply different pay scales, conditions, or facilities of employment according to the location of various plants or facilities

41.____

42. Data received by the Equal Employment Opportunity Commission from firms employing 100 or more people suggest that emphasis in the area of equal opportunity has shifted from one of detection of conscious discrimination to one of

    A. human resources utilization
    B. passive resistance
    C. unconscious discrimination
    D. education

42.____

43. According to surveys pertaining to equal employment opportunities, available information 43._____
indicates that discriminatory patterns in job placement of minority group members is

   A. higher in craft unions than in industrial unions
   B. greater in the East than in the West
   C. higher in new plants than in old plants
   D. higher among young executives than among old executives

44. The area of criticism on which Congress concentrated its attention in its recent investiga- 44._____
tions of testing was

   A. cultural bias
   B. depersonalization of the individual
   C. increase in *meritocracy*
   D. invasion of privacy

45. If accepted criteria of a profession are applied, which of the following work groupings 45._____
ranks LOWEST in the distinctiveness of its character as a profession?

   A. Social service or community work
   B. Managerial or administrative work
   C. Health or health services work
   D. Teaching or educational work

46. Surveys of factors contributing to job satisfaction indicate, according to employees, that 46._____
the factor having HIGHEST priority among those listed is

   A. opportunity for advancement
   B. good pay schedules
   C. concern for training employees for better job performance
   D. good work environment

47. Job enrichment is intended to increase employee motivation and interest by increasing 47._____
the accountability of employees for their work, by introducing more complex tasks, and
by granting authority to make job decisions.
A MAJOR hazard that ma.y result from application of such restructuring is to

   A. increase complaints of work pressure
   B. reduce the effectiveness of task specialization
   C. stimulate demand for salary increases
   D. limit the status of the immediate supervisor

48. Which of the following statements concerning performance appraisal systems is NOT 48._____
correct?
They

   A. require line management participation
   B. provide for periodic discussions of performance between the supervisor and the
      employee
   C. are used primarily to uncover employee weaknesses
   D. require supervisor training to assure uniform appraisals

49. In the forced-choice technique of performance evaluation, the rater is forced to judge   49._____
which of several alternative statements is most descriptive of an employee's performance. It forces the rater to discriminate on the basis of concrete aspects of a subordinate's work behavior rather than to rely on an impression of his total worth.
The one of the following which is NOT considered a value of this technique is that it

    A.   increases rater ability to produce a desired outcome
    B.   is relatively free of the usual pile-up at the top of the scale
    C.   tends to minimize subjective elements
    D.   produces results that correlate positively with other variables associated with effec-
        tive job performance

50. Of the following, the one which is NOT an advantage of the proper delegation of work by   50._____
a manager is that it

    A.   increases planning time
    B.   relieves the tension of seeing to details
    C.   increases the manager's familiarity with routine work
    D.   increases understanding of the responsibilities of subordinates

---

KEY (CORRECT ANSWERS)

1.	D	11.	C	21.	D	31.	C	41.	B
2.	D	12.	A	22.	C	32.	A	42.	A
3.	A	13.	B	23.	D	33.	B	43.	A
4.	C	14.	A	24.	D	34.	B	44.	D
5.	C	15.	D	25.	A	35.	B	45.	B
6.	B	16.	B	26.	A	36.	A	46.	A
7.	D	17.	C	27.	B	37.	B	47.	D
8.	B	18.	A	28.	C	38.	B	48.	C
9.	D	19.	C	29.	A	39.	D	49.	A
10.	C	20.	B	30.	D	40.	C	50.	C

EXAMINATION SECTION
TEST 1

DIRECTIONS: Each question or incomplete statement is followed by several suggested answers or completions. Select the one that BEST answers the question or completes the statement. *PRINT THE LETTER OF THE CORRECT ANSWER IN THE SPACE AT THE RIGHT.*

1. Competent civil service personnel cannot come just from initial employment on a competitive basis and equal pay for equal work.
   The one of the following additional factors which is of GREATEST importance in building up a body of competent civil service employees is

   A. analysis of work methods and introduction of streamlined procedures
   B. training for skill improvement and creating a sense of belonging
   C. rotation of employees from organization to organization in order to prevent stagnation
   D. treating personnel problems on a more impersonal basis in order to maintain an objective viewpoint
   E. recruiting for all higher positions from among the body of present employees

   1.____

2. A comment made by an employee about a training course was: *Half of the group seem to know what the course is about, the rest of us can't keep up with them.*
   The FUNDAMENTAL error in training methods to which this criticism points is

   A. insufficient student participation
   B. failure to develop a feeling of need or active want for the material being presented
   C. that the training session may be too long
   D. that no attempt may have been made to connect the new material with what was already known by any member of the group
   E. that insufficient provision has been made by the instructor for individual differences

   2.____

3. The one of the following which is NOT a major purpose of an employee suggestion plan is to

   A. provide an additional method by means of which an employee's work performance can be evaluated
   B. increase employee interest in the work of the organization
   C. provide an additional channel of communication between the employee and top management
   D. utilize to the greatest extent possible the ideas and proposals of employees
   E. provide a formal method for rewarding the occasional valuable idea

   3.____

4. The pay plan is a vital aspect of a duties classification. In fact, in most areas of personnel administration, pay plan and classification are synonymous.
   This statement is

   A. *correct* in general; while the two are not, in general, synonymous, the pay plan is such a vital aspect that without it the classification plan is meaningless and useless
   B. *not correct;* while the pay plan is a vital aspect of a classification plan, it is not the only one

   4.____

C. *correct* in general; pay plan and duties classification are simply two different aspects of the same problem - *equal pay for equal work*
D. *not correct;* although classification is usually a vital element of a pay plan, a pay plan is not essential to the preparation of a duties classification
E. *meaningless* unless the specific nature of the classification plan and the pay plan are set forth

5. The one of the following objectives which is MOST characteristic of intelligent personnel management is the desire to   5.____

    A. obtain competent employees, and having them to provide the climate which will be most conducive to superior performance, proper attitudes, and harmonious adjustments
    B. coordinate the activities of the workers in an organization so that the output will be maximized and cost minimized
    C. reduce the dependence of an organization on the sentiments, ambitions, and idiosyncracies of individual employees and thus advance the overall aims of the organization
    D. recruit employees who can be trained to subordinate their interests to the interests of the organization and to train them to do so
    E. mechanize the procedures involved so that problems of replacement and training are reduced to a minimum

6. An organizational structure which brings together, in a single work unit, work divisions which are non-homogeneous in work, in technology, or in purpose will tend to decrease the danger of friction.
This opinion is, in general,   6.____

    A. *correct;* individious comparisons tend to be made when everyone is doing the same thing
    B. *not correct;* a homogeneous organization tends to develop a strong competitive spirit among its employees
    C. *correct;* work which is non-homogeneous tends to be of greater interest to the employee, resulting in less friction
    D. *not correct;* persons performing the same type of work tend to work together more efficiently
    E. *correct;* the presence of different kinds of work permits better placement of employees, resulting in better morale

7. Of the following, the MOST accurate statement of current theory concerning the ultimate responsibility for employee training is that   7.____

    A. ultimate responsibility for training is best separated from responsibility for production and administration
    B. ultimate responsibility for training should be in the hands of a training specialist in the central personnel agency
    C. a committee of employees selected from the trainees should be given ultimate responsibility for the training program
    D. a departmental training specialist should be assigned ultimate responsibility for employee training
    E. each official should be ultimately responsible for the training of all employees under his direction

8. The BEST of the following ways to reduce the errors in supervisors' ratings of employee performance caused by variations in the application of the rating standards is to

    A. construct a method for translating each rating into a standard score
    B. inform each supervisor of the distribution of ratings expected in his unit
    C. review and change any rating which does not seem justified by the data presented by the rating supervisor
    D. arrange for practice sessions for supervisors at which rating standards will be applied and discussed
    E. confer with the supervisor when a case of disagreement is discovered between supervisor and review board

9. Which capsule description, among the following, constitutes an optimum arrangement of the hierarchical organization of a large-city central personnel agency?

    A. Three commissioners who appoint a Director of Personnel to carry out the administrative functions but who handle the quasi-judicial and quasi-legislative duties themselves
    B. A Director of Personnel and two Commissioners all three of whom participate in all aspects of the agency's functions
    C. A Director of Personnel who is responsible for making the final decision in all matters pertaining to personnel administration in a city
    D. A Director of Personnel who is the chief administrator and two Commissioners who, together with the Director, handle the quasi-judicial and quasi-legislative duties
    E. Three Commissioners who have review powers over the acts of the Director of Personnel who is appointed on the basis of a competitive examination

10. The one of the following which is a major objective expected to be gained by setting up a personnel council composed of representatives of the central personnel agency and departmental personnel officers is to

    A. provide an appeal board to which employees who feel grieved can appeal
    B. allow the departments to participate in making the day-to-day decisions faced by the central personnel agency
    C. prevent the departments from participating in making the day-to-day decisions faced by the central personnel agency
    D. establish good communications between the central personnel agency and the departments
    E. develop a broad base of responsibility for the actions of the central personnel agency

11. The one of the following which should be the starting point in the development of an accident reduction or prevention program is the

    A. institution of an interorganizational safety contest
    B. improvement of the conditions of work so that accidents are prevented
    C. inauguration of a safety education program to reduce accidents due to carelessness
    D. organization of unit safety committees to bring home the importance of safety to the individual worker
    E. determination of the number, character, and causes of accidents

12. An orientation program for a group of new employees would NOT usually include 12.____

    A. a description of the physical layout of the organization
    B. a statement of the rules pertaining to leave, lateness, overtime, and so forth
    C. detailed instruction on the job each employee is to perform
    D. an explanation of the lines of promotion
    E. a talk on the significance of the role the department plays in the governmental structure

13. The device of temporary assignment of an employee to the duties of the higher position is sometimes used to determine promotability.
The use of this procedure, especially for top positions, is 13.____

    A. *desirable;* no test or series of tests can measure fitness to the same extent as actual trial on the job
    B. *undesirable;* the organization will not have a responsible head during the trial period
    C. *desirable;* employees who are on trial tend to operate with greater efficiency
    D. *undesirable;* the organization would tend to deteriorate if no one of the candidates for the position was satisfactory
    E. *desirable;* the procedure outlined is simpler and less expensive than any series of tests

14. Frequently, when accumulating data for a salary standardization study, the salaries for certain basic positions are compared with the salaries paid in other agencies, public and private.
The one of the following which would MOST usually be considered one of these basic positions is 14.____

    A. Office Manager   B. Administrative Assistant
    C. Chief Engineer   D. Junior Typist
    E. Chemist

15. The emphasis in public personnel administration during recent years has been less on the 15.____

    A. need for the elimination of the spoils system and more on the development of policy and techniques of administration that contribute to employee selection and productivity
    B. development of policy and techniques of administration that contribute to employee selection and productivity and more on the need for the elimination of the spoils system
    C. human relation aspects of personnel administration and more on the technical problems of classification and placement
    D. problems of personnel administration of governmental units in the United States and more on those of international organizations
    E. problems of personnel administration in international organizations and more on those of governmental units in the United States

16. The recommendation has been made that explicit information be made available to all city employees concerning the procedure to be followed when appealing from a performance rating.
To put this recommendation into effect would be 16.____

A. *desirable*, primarily because employees would tend to have greater confidence in the performance rating system
B. *undesirable*, primarily because a greater number of employees would submit appeals with no merit
C. *desirable*, primarily because the additional publicity would spotlight the performance rating system
D. *undesirable*, primarily because all appeals should be treated as confidential matters and all efforts to make them public should be defeated
E. *desirable*, primarily because committing the appeal procedure to paper would tend to standardize it

17. The one of the following which in most cases is the BEST practical measure of the merits of the overall personnel policies of one organization as compared to the policies of similar organizations in the same area is the 17._____

A. extent to which higher positions in the hierarchy are filled by career employees
B. degree of loyalty and enthusiasm manifested by the work force
C. rate at which replacements must be made in order to maintain the work force
D. percentage of employees who have joined labor unions and the militancy of these unions
E. scale of salaries

18. Classification may most properly be viewed as the building of a structure. The fundamental unit in the classification structure is the 18._____

A. assignment   B. position   C. service
D. rank   E. grade

19. The one of the following which is NOT usually included in a class specification is 19._____

A. a definition of the duties and responsibilities covered
B. the class title
C. a description of the recruitment method to be used
D. a statement of typical tasks performed
E. the statement of minimum qualifications necessary to perform the work

20. The one of the following which is usually NOT considered part of a classification survey is 20._____

A. grouping positions on the basis of similarities
B. preparing job specifications
C. analyzing and recording specific job duties
D. adjusting job duties to employee qualifications
E. allocating individual positions to classes

21. The one of the following which is MOST generally accepted as a prerequisite to the development of a sound career service is 21._____

A. agreement to accept for all higher positions the senior eligible employee
B. the recruitment of an adequate proportion of beginning employees who will eventually be capable of performing progressively more difficult duties
C. strict adherence to the principle of competitive promotion from within for all positions above the entrance level

D. the development of a program of periodically changing an employee's duties in order to prevent stagnation
E. the existence of administrators who can stimulate employees and keep their production high

22. The determination of the fitness of a person to fill a position solely on the basis of his experience is

    22.____

  A. *desirable;* experience is the best test of aptitude for a position when it is rated properly
  B. *undesirable;* the applicant may not be giving correct factual information in regard to his experience
  C. *desirable;* a uniform rating key can be applied to evaluate experience
  D. *undesirable;* it is difficult to evaluate from experience records how much the applicant has gained from his experience
  E. *desirable;* there will be more applicants for a position if no written or oral tests are required

23. The performance rating standards in a city department have been criticized by its employees as unfair.
The one of the following procedures which would probably be HOST effective in reducing this criticism is to

    23.____

  A. publish a detailed statement showing how the standards were arrived at
  B. provide for participation by employee representatives in revising the standards
  C. allow individual employees to submit written statements about the standards employed
  D. arrange for periodic meetings of the entire staff at which the standards are discussed
  E. appoint a review board consisting of senior supervisory employees to reconsider the standards

24. The statement has been made that personnel administration is the MOST fundamental and important task of the head of any organization.
This statement is based, for the most part, on the fact that

    24.____

  A. success or failure of an organization to reach its objectives depends on the attitudes and abilities of the people in the organization
  B. the influence of personnel administration on organization success varies in proportion to the number, the complexity, and the rarity of the virtues and qualities that are requisite to superior performance of the tasks involved
  C. a sound philosophy of personnel administration emphasizes the basic objective of superior service over any other consideration
  D. relative autonomy is permitted each department, particularly with respect to the handling of personnel
  E. diversity of personnel practices as to salaries, hours, etc., leads to poor morale

25. The requirement imposed by most civil service laws in the United States that tests shall be *practical in character and deal in so far as possible with the actual duties of the position,* has led to a wide use of

    25.____

A. tests of social outlook
B. aptitude tests
C. achievement tests
D. objective tests
E. oral tests

26. In general, the one of the following which is the first step in the construction of a test for the selection of personnel is to   26.____

   A. determine what the duties of the position to be filled are
   B. investigate the relationships among abilities and capacities required for success in the position to be filled
   C. study examinations which have been given in the' past for similar positions
   D. evaluate existing examining instruments to determine their adequacy for making the desired selection
   E. set up the outline and start preliminary preparation of the examining instruments

27. The one of the following situations which is MOST likely to result from a too highly speci-fied assignment or definition of responsibility is that   27.____

   A. there will be no standard against which to measure the efficiency of the organiza-tion
   B. duplication and overlapping of functions will be encouraged
   C. sufficient channels to collect, synthesize, and coordinate all performances may not be provided
   D. essential tasks which have not been explicitly mentioned in the assignment may not get done
   E. there will be a tendency to overlook the need for training

28. Assume that you are interviewing a new entrance level clerical employee for the purpose of determining where he would be best placed.
In making your determination, the characteristic to which you should give GREATEST weight is the employee's   28.____

   A. interest in the jobs you describe to him
   B. mechanical aptitude
   C. poise and self-assurance
   D. fluency of verbal expression
   E. educational background and his hobbies

29. The use of the probationary period in the public service has become an approved prac-tice especially where state tenure laws guarantee long-term continuous employment. Of the following, the MOST important use of the probationary period is that it   29.____

   A. provides supervisory contact which will help the new employee regardless of reten-tion at the end of the probationary period
   B. supplies confirming evidence of academic and cultural fitness not measurable in formal test procedures
   C. introduces the new employee to the office and the work situation which conditions future performance
   D. provides the new employee with a sound basis for self-improvement
   E. reveals aspects of performance and attitude toward the job not adequately mea-sured by formal examination

30. The first prerequisite to the formulation of any compensation plan for a public agency is   30.____
the collection and analysis of certain basic data.
Data are NOT usually collected for this purpose in regard to

    A. working conditions in the agency
    B. the wage paid in the agency at present
    C. labor turnover in the agency
    D. the cost of living in the area
    E. the age and sex distribution of the employees

31. The one of the following personnel administration techniques which when properly uti-   31.____
lized will yield information concerning current training needs of an organization is the

    A. classification plan   B. performance rating
    C. personnel register   D. compensation plan
    E. employee handbook

32. In administering the activities of a personnel office with a staff of fifteen employees,   32.____
including seven personnel technicians, the personnel officer should

    A. delegate full authority and responsibility to each staff member and discharge those
       who do not meet his standards
    B. endeavor to keep tab on the work of each individual on his staff
    C. make sure each job is being done properly or do it himself
    D. plan work programs, make assignments, and check on performance
    E. concern himself only with major policies and expect subordinates to carry out
       actual functions

33. The one of the following factors which is MOST influential in determining the proportion   33.____
of qualified applicants who refuse public employment when offered is the

    A. interim between application and offer of a position
    B. specific nature of the duties of the position
    C. general nature of economic conditions at the time when the position is offered
    D. salary paid
    E. general undesirable nature of public employment

34. A placement officer in a department follows the procedure of consulting the supervisor of   34.____
the unit in which a vacancy exists concerning the kind of worker he wants before
attempting to fill the vacancy.
This procedure is, in general,

    A. *undesirable;* it makes the selection process dependent on the whim of the supervi-
       sor
    B. *desirable;* it will make for a more effectively working organization
    C. *undesirable;* if the kind of worker the supervisor wants is not available, he will be
       dissatisfied
    D. *desirable;* the more people who are consulted about a matter of this kind, the more
       chance there is that no mistake will be made
    E. *undesirable;* the wishes of the worker as well as those of the supervisor should be
       taken into consideration

35. In a large organization, proper recruitment is not possible without the existence of an   35._____
effective position classification system.
The one of the following which BEST explains why this is the case is that otherwise
effective means of determining the capabilities and characteristics of prospective
employees are of little value

    A. unless these are related to the salary scale and current economic conditions
    B. without a knowledge of the essential character of the work to be performed in each
position
    C. where no attempt to classify the different recruitment approaches has been made
in advance
    D. if there has been no attempt made to obtain the cooperation of the employees
involved
    E. to personnel officers who tend to place new employees in positions without refer-
ence to capabilities

36. The recommendation has been made that a departmental grievance board be set up,   36._____
which would handle all employee grievances from their inception to conclusion.
Of the following comments for and against the acceptance of this recommendation, the
one which is NOT valid is that it is

    A. *desirable,* primarily because it will remove a constant source of friction between
supervisor and employee and place the problem in the hands of an objective board
    B. *undesirable,* primarily because handling grievances is an integral part of the super-
visory process and the immediate supervisor must be afforded the opportunity to
deal with the situation
    C. *desirable,* primarily because no supervisor will have to determine whether he has
been unfair to one of his subordinates and no subordinate will have a grievance
    D. *desirable,* primarily because the handling of grievances will tend to be expedited
as the board will have only one function
    E. *undesirable,* primarily because the handling of grievances will tend to be delayed
as the board will not have all the necessary information available

37. The one of the following which is frequently given as a major argument against a tightly   37._____
knit promotion-from-within policy is that

    A. it takes too long for an employee in the lower grades to reach the top
    B. all persons both in and out of the government are equally entitled to civil service
jobs
    C. persons are placed in executive jobs who are too well acquainted with the existing
organization
    D. it leads to the presence in executive jobs of clerks who still operate as clerks
    E. it is not desirable to guarantee to all employees promotion to new responsibilities
from time to time

38. Of the following factors which are influential in determining which employment a young   38._____
man or woman will choose, government employ is generally considered superior in

    A. incentives to improve efficiency
    B. opportunities to move into other similar organizations
    C. prestige and recognition
    D. leave and retirement benefits
    E. salaries

39. Training programs, to be fully effective, should be concerned not only with the acquisition   39.____
or improvement of skills but also with

  A. employee attitude and will to work
  B. the personality problems of the individual employees
  C. time and motion studies for the development of new procedures
  D. the recruitment of the best persons available to fill a given position
  E. such theoretical background material as is deemed necessary

Questions 40-45.

DIRECTIONS: Questions 40 through 45 are to be answered on the basis of the following
paragraphs.

Plan 1   Hire broadly qualified people, work out their assignments from time to time to suit
the needs of the enterprise and aptitudes of individuals. Let their progress and
recognition be based on the length and overall quality of the service, regardless of
the significance of individual assignments which they periodically assume.

Plan 2   Hire experts and assign them well-defined duties. Their compensation, for the
most part, should be dependent on the duties performed.

40. For Plan 1 to be successful, there must be assured, to a much greater extent than for   40.____
Plan 2, the existence of

  A. a well-developed training program
  B. a widely publicized recruitment program
  C. in general, better working conditions
  D. more skilled administrators
  E. a greater willingness to work together toward a common goal

41. Plan 1 would tend to develop employees who were   41.____

  A. dissatisfied because of the impossibility of advancing rapidly to positions of impor-
tance
  B. conversant only with problems in the particular field in which they were employed
  C. in general, not satisfied with the work they perform
  D. intensely competitive
  E. able to perform a variety of functions

42. Large governmental organizations in the United States tend, in general, to use Plan   42.____

  A. 1
  B. 2
  C. 1 for technical positions and Plan 2 for clerical positions
  D. 2 for administrative positions and Plan 1 for clerical and technical positions
  E. 1 for office machine operators and Plan 2 for technical positions

43. In organizations which operate on the basis of Plan 1, placement of a man in the proper job after selection is much more difficult than in those which operate on the basis of Plan 2.
This statement is, in general,

    A. *correct;* the organization would have only specific positions open and generalists would be forced into technical positions
    B. *not correct;* specific aptitudes and abilities would tend to be determined in advance as would be the case with Plan 2
    C. *correct;* it is much more difficult to determine specific aptitudes and abilities than general qualifications
    D. *not correct;* placement would be based on the needs of the organization, consequently only a limited number of positions would be available
    E. *correct;* the selection is not on the basis of specific aptitudes and abilities

43.____

44. Administration in an organization operating on the basis of Plan 1 would tend to be less flexible than one operating on the basis of Plan 2.
This statement is, in general,

    A. *correct;* recruitment of experts permits rapid expansion
    B. *not correct;* the absence of well-defined positions permits wide and rapid recruitment without an extensive selection period
    C. *correct;* well-defined positions allow for replacement on an assembly-line basis without an extensive breaking-in period and thus permits greater flexibility
    D. *not correct;* Plan 1 presents greater freedom in movement of individuals from one position to another and in re-defining positions according to capabilities of employees and the needs of the moment
    E. *correct;* Plan 1 presents greater freedom in adjusting an organizational structure to unexpected stresses since the clear definition of duties shows where the danger points are

44.____

45. To a greater extent than Plan 2, Plan 1 leads to conflict and overlapping in administrative operations.
In general, this is the case because

    A. employees paid on the basis of duties performed tend to be more conscious of overlapping operations and tend to limit their activities
    B. experts refuse to accept responsibilities in fields other than their own
    C. the lack of carefully defined positions may conceal many points at which coordination and reconciliation are necessary
    D. there tends to be more pressure for *empire building* where prestige is measured solely in terms of assignment
    E. there is less need, under Plan 1, to define lines of responsibility and authority and consequently conflict will arise

45.____

46. Some organizations interview employees who resign or are discharged.
This procedure is USUALLY

    A. of great value in reducing labor turnover and creating good will toward the organization
    B. of little or no value as the views of incompetent or disgruntled employees are of questionable validity

46.____

C.   dangerous; it gives employees who are leaving an organization the opportunity to pay off old scores
D.   of great value in showing the way to more efficient methods of production and the establishment of higher work norms
E.   dangerous; it may lead to internal friction as operating departments believe that it is not the function of the personnel office to check on operations

47.   The one of the following which is the MOST common flaw in the administration of an employee performance rating system is the   47._____

A.   failure to explain the objectives of the system to employees
B.   lack of safeguards to prevent supervisors from rating employees down for personal reasons
C.   tendency for rating supervisors to rate their employees much too leniently
D.   fact that employees are aware of the existence of the system
E.   increasing number of committees and boards required

48.   As a result of its study of the operations of the Federal government, the Hoover Commission recommended that, for purposes of reduction in force, employees be ranked from the standpoint of their overall usefulness to the agency in question.   48._____
The one of the following which is a major disadvantage of this proposal is that it would probably result in

A.   efficient employees becoming indifferent to the social problems posed
B.   a sense of insecurity on the part of employees which might tend to lower efficiency
C.   the retention of employees who are at or just past their peak performance
D.   the retention of generalists rather than specialists
E.   the loss of experience in the agency, as ability rather than knowledge will be the criterion

49.   A personnel officer checking the turnover rate in his department found that, over a period of five years, the rate at which engineers left the organization was exactly the same as the rate at which junior clerks left the department.   49._____
This information tends to indicate

A.   that something may be amiss with the organization; the rate for engineers under ordinary circumstances should be higher than for clerks
B.   that the organization is in good shape; neither the technical nor clerical aspects are being overemphasized
C.   nothing which would be of value in determining the state of the organization
D.   that the organization is in good shape; working conditions, in general, are equivalent for all employees
E.   that something may be amiss with the organization; the turnover rate for engineers under ordinary circumstances should be lower than for clerks

50.   Of the following, the MOST essential feature of a grievance procedure is that   50._____

A.   those who appeal be assured of expert counsel
B.   the administration have opportunity to review cases early in the procedure
C.   it afford assurance that those who use it will not be discriminated against
D.   general grievances be publicized
E.   it be simple to administer

KEY (CORRECT ANSWERS)

1.	B	11.	E	21.	B	31.	B	41.	E
2.	E	12.	C	22.	D	32.	D	42.	B
3.	A	13.	A	23.	B	33.	A	43.	E
4.	D	14.	D	24.	A	34.	B	44.	D
5.	A	15.	A	25.	C	35.	B	45.	C
6.	D	16.	A	26.	A	36.	B	46.	A
7.	E	17.	C	27.	D	37.	D	47.	C
8.	D	18.	B	28.	A	38.	D	48.	B
9.	D	19.	C	29.	E	39.	A	49.	E
10.	D	20.	D	30.	E	40.	A	50.	C

TEST 2

DIRECTIONS: Each question or incomplete statement is followed by several suggested answers or completions. Select the one that BEST answers the question or completes the statement. *PRINT THE LETTER OF THE CORRECT ANSWER IN THE SPACE AT THE RIGHT.*

1. In which of the following fields could two or more groups duplicating each other's work USUALLY be best justified?   1.____

   A. Accounting
   B. Personnel
   C. Public relations
   D. Research and development
   E. Systems and procedures

2. Which of the following statements is MOST nearly accurate? A span of control   2.____

   A. of 5 people is better than that of 10 people
   B. of 5 people may be better or worse than that of 10 people
   C. of 5 people is worse than that of 10 people
   D. is rarely over 20 minutes at any one time
   E. means the same as the scalar system

3. A linear responsibility chart is   3.____

   A. a graphical method of showing each sub-project making up a total project with the time it takes to complete each
   B. a graphical method of showing jobs, functions, and, by the use of appropriate symbols, the relationship of each job to each function
   C. a graphical method of solving linear equations used in doing Operations Research
   D. a new method of procedures analysis which makes it possible to focus on both the employees and the equipment they use
   E. another name for a special organization chart

4. An administrator of a public agency is faced with the problem of deciding which of two   4.____
   divisions should be responsible for the statistical reporting of the agency. This work is now located in one of them but each of the two division chiefs believes that the work should be located within his division because of its relationship to other activities under his supervision. The Organization Planning Section is located in one of the two divisions. Assuming that in this situation the administrator can select any one of the following courses of action, the BEST for him to take would be to

   A. assign a staff member from the Organization Planning Section to study the problem, who for the duration of the assignment would report directly to the administrator
   B. assign staff from the Organization Planning Section to study the problem
   C. assign the statistical work to the other division for a trial period because of the problems which exist under the present arrangement
   D. call in an outside consultant or refer it to a competent staff employee not assigned to the divisions involved
   E. leave the organization as it is because the advantages of a change are not entirely clear to all concerned

5. The problem of whether office services such as filing, duplicating, and stenography should be centralized or decentralized arises in every business organization.
   One advantage of decentralizing these services is that

    5.____

    A. greater facility exists in such matters as finding correspondence
    B. greater flexibility exists in rotating workers during vacations
    C. higher production is attained at a lower cost per unit
    D. knowledge of the purpose and use of work acts as an incentive for production
    E. reduction in investment results from the use of less machinery

6. Research to date on the relationship between productivity and morale shows that

    6.____

    A. high productivity and high morale nearly always go together
    B. high productivity and low morale nearly always go together
    C. low productivity and high morale nearly always go together
    D. low productivity and low morale nearly always go together
    E. there is no clear relationship between productivity and morale

7. Which one of the following statements BEST describes *work measurement* as commonly used in government?
   It is

    7.____

    A. a method of establishing an equitable relationship between volume of work performed and manpower utilized
    B. a new technique which may be substituted for traditional accounting methods
    C. the amount of work turned out by an organization in a given time period
    D. the same as the work count, as used in Work Simplification
    E. the same as time-motion study

8. Critics of work measurement have contended that any increase in production is more than offset by deterioration in standards of quality or service.
   The BEST answer to this charge is to

    8.____

    A. argue that increases in production have not been offset by decreased quality
    B. define work units in terms of both quality and quantity
    C. ignore it
    D. point out that statistical quality control can be used to control quality
    E. point out that work measurement is not concerned with quality, and hence that the argument is irrelevant

9. When it is determined that a given activity or process is so intangible that it cannot be reflected adequately by
   a work unit, it is BEST for a work measurement system to

    9.____

    A. combine that activity with others that are measurable
    B. discuss the activity only in narrative reports
    C. exclude it from the work measurement system
    D. include only the time devoted to that activity or process
    E. select the best available work unit, as better than none

10. Which one of the following is frequently referred to as the father of Statistical Quality   10._____
    Control?

    A. Ralph M. Barnes   B. John M. Pfiffner
    C. Benjamin Selekman   D. Walter A. Shewhart
    E. Donald C. Stone

11. Which one of the following BEST explains the use and value of the *upper control limit*   11._____
    (and *lower control limit* where applicable) in Statistical Quality Control?
    It

    A. automatically keeps production under control
    B. indicates that unit costs are too high or too low
    C. is useful as a training device for new workers
    D. tells what pieces to discard or errors to correct
    E. tells when assignable causes as distinguished from chance causes are at work

12. A manager skilled in human relations can BEST be defined as one who   12._____

    A. can identify interpersonal problems and work out solutions to them
    B. can persuade people to do things his way
    C. gets along well with people and has many friends
    D. plays one role with his boss, another with his subordinates, and a third with his
       peers
    E. treats everyone fairly

13. The BEST way to secure efficient management is to   13._____

    A. allow staff agencies to solve administrative problems
    B. equip line management to solve its own problems
    C. get employees properly classified and trained
    D. prescribe standard operating procedures
    E. set up a board of control

14. The composition of the work force in American government and industry is changing.   14._____
    There has been an increase in the proportion of white collar to blue collar employees and
    an increase in the proportion of higher educated to lower educated employees.
    This change will MOST likely result in

    A. a more simplified forms control system
    B. closer supervision of employees
    C. further decentralization of decision-making
    D. more employee grievances
    E. organization by process instead of purpose

15. In which of the following professional journals would you be MOST apt to find articles on   15._____
    organization theory?

    A. Administrative Science Quarterly
    B. Factory Management and Maintenance
    C. Harvard Business Review
    D. O and M
    E. Public Administration Review

16. Which of the following organizations is MOST noted for its training courses in various management subjects?

    A. American Management Association
    B. American Political Science Association
    C. American Society for Public Administration
    D. Society for the Advancement of Management
    E. Systems and Procedures Association

16.____

17. A *performance budget* puts emphasis on

    A. achieving greatest economy
    B. expenditures for salaries, travel, rent, supplies, etc.
    C. revenues rather than on expenditures
    D. tables of organization or staffing patterns
    E. what is accomplished, e.g., number of applications processed, trees planted, buildings inspected, etc.

17.____

18. Which of the following statements MOST accurately defines *Operations Research?*

    A. A highly sophisticated reporting system used in the analysis of management problems
    B. A specialized application of electronic data processing in the analysis of management problems
    C. Research on operating problems
    D. Research on technological problems
    E. The application of sophisticated mathematical tools to the analysis of management problems

18.____

19. Which of the following characteristics of a system would MOST likely lead to the conclusion that manual methods should be used rather than punch card equipment?

    A. High volume
    B. Low volume but complex computations
    C. Operations of a fixed sequence
    D. Relatively simple work
    E. Repetitive work

19.____

20. Assume that a computer with typing software costs $1100 and an electric typewriter costs $300. Except for speed of production, assume that in all other pertinent respects they are the same, including a life expectancy of 10 years each.
What is the approximate amount of time $7.40 per hour typist must save and re-invest in work to have her computer recoup the difference in purchase price?

    A. 11 hours annually   B. 110 hours annually
    C. 550 hours annually   D. 1100 hours annually
    E. One hour a day

20.____

21. The principal justification for using office machines to replace hand labor is to   21.____

    A. achieve automation   B. eliminate errors
    C. increase productivity   D. make work easier
    E. reduce labor problems

22. An analog computer is one which   22.____

    A. is classified as *medium* size
    B. is used primarily for solving scientific and engineering problems rather than for data processing
    C. operates on the principle of creating a physical, often electrical, analogy of the mathematical problem to be solved
    D. uses transistors rather than vacuum tubes
    E. works on the basis of logarithms

23. The binary numbering system used in computers is one which   23.____

    A. is much more complicated than the usual decimal numbering system
    B. uses a radix or base of 8
    C. uses letters of the alphabet rather than numerical digits
    D. uses only two digits, 0 and 1
    E. uses the customary ten digits, 0 through 9

24. An electronic computer performs various arithmetic operations by   24.____

    A. adding and subtracting
    B. adding, subtracting, dividing, and multiplying
    C. Boolean algebra
    D. multiplying and dividing
    E. all operations listed in B and C

25. The MOST effective basis for an analysis of the flow of work in a large governmental agency is the   25.____

    A. analysis of descriptions written by employees
    B. discussion of routines with selected employees
    C. discussion of operations with supervisors
    D. initiation of a series of general staff meetings to discuss operational procedures
    E. observation of actual operations

26. The BEST reason for prescribing definite procedures for certain work in an organization is to   26.____

    A. enable supervisor to keep *on top of* details of work
    B. enable work to be processed speedily and consistently
    C. facilitate incorporation of new policies
    D. prevent individual discretion
    E. reduce training periods

27. Which one of the following is the MOST important difference between clerks in small
offices and those in large offices?
Clerks in

    A. large offices are less closely supervised
    B. large offices have more freedom to exercise originality in their work
    C. small offices are more restricted by standardized procedures
    D. small offices are more specialized in their duties
    E. small offices need a greater variety of clerical skills

27.____

28. After taking the necessary steps to analyze a situation, an employee reaches a decision
which is reviewed by his supervisor and found to be incorrect.
Of the following possible methods of dealing with this incident, the MOST constructive
for the employee would be for the supervisor to

    A. correct the decision and give the employee an explanation
    B. correct the decision and suggest more detailed analysis in the future
    C. help the employee discover what is wrong with the basis for decision
    D. set up a temporary control on this type of decision until the employee demon-
strates he can handle it
    E. suggest that the employee review future cases of this type with him before reach-
ing a decision

28.____

29. Which one of the following is NOT a purpose ordinarily served by charts?

    A. Aid in training employees
    B. Assist in presenting and selling recommendations
    C. Detect gaps or discrepancies in data collected
    D. Put facts in proper relationships to each other
    E. Show up problems of human relationships

29.____

30. Which of the following descriptive statements does NOT constitute a desirable standard
in evaluating an administrative sequence or series of tasks having a definite objective?

    A. All material should be routed as directly as possible to reduce the cost of time and
motion.
    B. Each form must clear the section chief before going to another section.
    C. Each task should be assigned to the lowest-ranking employee who can perform it
adequately.
    D. Each task should contribute positively to the basic purpose of the sequence.
    E. Similar tasks should be combined.

30.____

31. Which one of the following is NOT a principle of motion economy?

    A. Continuous curved motions are preferable to straight-line motions involving sud-
den and sharp changes in direction.
    B. Motions of the arms should be made in the same direction and should be made
simultaneously.
    C. The hands should be relieved of all work that can be performed more advanta-
geously by the feet.
    D. The two hands should begin and complete their motions at the same time.
    E. Two or more tools should be combined whenever possible.

31.____

32. Generally, the first step in the measurement of relative efficiency of office employees engaged in machine operation is the
    32._____

    A. analysis of the class of positions involved to determine the duties and responsibilities and minimum qualifications necessary for successful job performance
    B. analysis of those skills which make for difference in the production of various employees
    C. development of a service rating scale which can be scored accurately
    D. development of a standard unit of production that can be widely applied and that will give comparable data
    E. selection of an appropriate sampling of employees whose duties involve the specific factors to be measured

33. In the course of a survey, a disgruntled employee of Unit A comes to your office with an offer to *tell all* about Unit B, where he used to work.
    You should
    33._____

    A. listen to him but ignore any statements he makes
    B. listen to him carefully, but verify his assertions before acting on them
    C. make him speak to you in the presence of the persons he is criticizing
    D. reprimand him for not minding his own business
    E. report him to the security officer

34. Combining several different procedures into a single flow of work would MOST likely achieve which of the following advantages?
    34._____

    A. Better teamwork
    B. Higher quality decisions
    C. Improved morale
    D. Reduced fluctuations in workload
    E. Reduced problems of control

35. After conducting a systems survey in the Personnel Division you find that there is not sufficient work in the Division to keep a recently hired employee gainfully employed.
    The BEST solution to this problem is usually to
    35._____

    A. lay off the employee with a full month's salary
    B. leave the employee in the Division because the workload may increase
    C. leave the employee in the Personnel Division, but assign him overflow work from other divisions
    D. reassign the employee when an appropriate opening occurs elsewhere in the organization
    E. request the employee to resign so that no unfavorable references will appear on his personnel record

36. You are making a study of a central headquarters office which processes claims received   36.____
from a number of regional offices. You notice the following problems: some employees
are usually busy while others assigned to the same kind of work in the same grade have
little to do; high-level professional people frequently spend considerable time searching
for files in the file room.
Which of the following charts would be MOST useful to record and analyze the data
needed to help solve these problems?
_____ chart.

    A. forms distribution   B. layout
    C. operation   D. process
    E. work distribution

37. A *therblig* is BEST defined as a   37.____

    A. follower of Frederick W. Taylor
    B. small element or task of an operation used in time–motion study
    C. special type of accounting machine
    D. type of curve used in charting certain mathematical relationships
    E. unit for measuring the effectiveness of air conditioning

38. One of the following advantages which is LEAST likely to accrue to a large organization   38.____
as a result of establishing a centralized typing and stenographic unit is that

    A. less time is wasted
    B. morale of the stenographers increases
    C. the stenographers receive better training
    D. wages are more consistent
    E. work is more equally distributed

39. In the communications process, the work *noise* is used to refer to   39.____

    A. anything that interferes with the message between transmitter and receiver
    B. meaningless communications
    C. the amplitude of verbal communication
    D. the level of general office and environmental sounds other than specific verbal
       communications
    E. the product of the grapevine

40. Which of the following is NOT an advantage of oral instructions as compared with written   40.____
instructions when dealing with a small group?

    A. Oral instructions are more adaptable to complex orders
    B. Oral instructions can be changed more easily and quickly.
    C. Oral instructions facilitate exchange of information between the order giver and
       order receiver.
    D. Oral instructions make it easier for order giver and order receiver.
    E. The oral medium is suitable for instructions that will be temporary.

41. The employee opinion or attitude survey has for some time been accepted as a valuable 41.____
    communications device.
    Of the following, the benefit which is LEAST likely to occur from the use of such a sur-
    vey is:

    A. A clearer view of employee understanding of management policies is obtained
    B. Improved morale may result
    C. Information useful for supervisory and executive development is obtained
    D. The reasons why management policies were adopted are clarified
    E. Useful comparisons can be made between organization units

42. Which of the following is the MOST important principle to remember in preparing written 42.____
    reports that are to be submitted to a superior?

    A. Avoid mentioning in writing errors or mistakes
    B. Include human interest anecdotes
    C. Put all information into graphical or tabular form
    D. Report everything that has happened
    E. Report results in relation to plan

43. In conducting an electronic data processing study, with which one of the following should 43.____
    you be LEAST concerned?

    A. Computer characteristics; i.e., word length requirements, type storage characteris-
       tics, etc.
    B. Data collection requirements
    C. Methods used by other governmental jurisdictions
    D. System input/output requirements and volume
    E. System integration and flow of work

44. The MOST significant difference between a random access and a sequential type data 44.____
    processing computer system is

    A. Generally, a random access system has lower *locating* or access times
    B. Random access provides the potential for processing data on a *first come–first
       served* basis without the necessity of batching or pre-arranging the data in some
       sequence
    C. Random access systems are more often disk type storage systems
    D. Random access systems can operate more easily in conjunction with sequential
       tape or card oriented computer systems
    E. Random access systems have larger storage capacities

45. The most effective leader would MOST likely be one who 45.____

    A. is able to use a variety of leadership styles depending on the circumstances
    B. issues clear, forceful directives
    C. knows the substance of the work better than any of his subordinates
    D. supervises his subordinates closely
    E. uses democratic methods

46. One large office is a more efficient operating unit than the same number of square feet   46.____
    split into smaller offices.
    Of the following, the one that does NOT support this statement is:

    A. Better light and ventilation are possible
    B. Changes in layout are less apt to be made thus avoiding disruption of work flow
    C. Communication between individual employees is more direct
    D. Space is more fully utilized
    E. Supervision and control are more easily maintained

47. The major purpose for adopting specific space standards is to   47.____

    A. allocate equal space to employees doing the same kind of work
    B. cut costs
    C. keep space from becoming a status symbol
    D. prevent empire–building
    E. provide an accurate basis for charging for space allocated to each organization
       unit

48. The modular concept in office space planning is   48.____

    A. a method of pre-planning office space for economical use
    B. expensive because it complicates the air conditioning and electrical systems
    C. outdated because it lacks flexibility
    D. used as a basis for planning future space requirements
    E. used primarily for executive offices

49. Which one of the following statements is NOT correct?   49.____

    A. A general conference or committee room may eliminate the need for a number of
       private offices.
    B. In designing office space the general trend is toward the use of a standard color
       scheme.
    C. Private offices should be constructed in such a way as to avoid cutting off natural
       light and ventilation.
    D. Private offices result in a larger investment in equipment and furnishings.
    E. Transparent or translucent glass can be used in the upper portion of the partition
       for private offices.

50. Which one of the following is NOT a good general rule of communications in an organiza-   50.____
    tion?

    A. All supervisors should know the importance of communications.
    B. Oral communications are better than written where persuasion is needed.
    C. People should be told facts that make them feel they *belong*.
    D. The grapevine should be eliminated.
    E. The supervisor should hear information before his subordinates.

KEY (CORRECT ANSWERS)

1.	D	11.	E	21.	C	31.	B	41.	D
2.	B	12.	A	22.	C	32.	D	42.	E
3.	B	13.	B	23.	D	33.	B	43.	C
4.	D	14.	C	24.	A	34.	D	44.	B
5.	D	15.	A	25.	E	35.	D	45.	A
6.	E	16.	A	26.	B	36.	E	46.	B
7.	A	17.	E	27.	E	37.	B	47.	A
8.	B	18.	E	28.	C	38.	B	48.	A
9.	D	19.	B	29.	E	39.	A	49.	B
10.	D	20.	A	30.	B	40.	A	50.	D

EXAMINATION SECTION
TEST 1

DIRECTIONS: Each question or incomplete statement is followed by several suggested answers or completions. Select the one that BEST answers the question or completes the statement. *PRINT THE LETTER OF THE CORRECT ANSWER IN THE SPACE AT THE RIGHT.*

1. Willful violations of OSHA provisions by a corporate employer are punishable by maximum fines of up to_____ upon criminal conviction.   1.____

   A. $5,000   B. $50,000   C. $250,000   D. $500,000

2. Which of the following occurs when employees perceive too narrow a difference between their own pay and that of other colleagues?   2.____

   A. Pay compression   B. Wage inflation
   C. Pay survey   D. Skills gap

3. A local union typically engages in each of the following activities EXCEPT   3.____

   A. administering contracts   B. training union leaders
   C. organizing campaigns   D. collecting dues

4. Under existing laws or mandates, affirmative action programs are mandated for the hiring practices of   4.____

   A. public educational institutions
   B. government contractors
   C. federal agencies
   D. all of the above

5. In evaluating a training program, a human resources professional wants specifically to learn whether the knowledge, skills, or abilities learned in training led to an employee's improved performance on the job. Her evaluation of the program would test for _____ validity.   5.____

   A. training   B. transfer
   C. intraorganizational   D. interorganizational

6. In human resources, *methods study* is concerned with   6.____

   A. the way in which work is distributed among personnel
   B. determining the most efficient way of doing a task or job
   C. determining the minimum number of employees needed to complete a task or job
   D. the criteria used to hire employees

7. Which of the following is/are advantages associated with internal recruiting?   7.____
   I. It offers loyal employees a fair chance at promotion.
   II. It helps protect trade secrets.
   III. It encourages new ideas and competition.
   The CORRECT answer is:

   A. I *only*   B. III *only*   C. I, II   D. II, III

8. In the vocabulary of job analysis, coordinated and aggregated series of work elements   8.____
   that are used to produce a specific output are referred to as

   A. positions   B. jobs   C. chores   D. tasks

9. During the personnel selection process, human resource professionals sometimes use   9.____
   selection tests that are designed to have what is called *predictive validity.* The primary
   drawback to using this type of assessment is that

   A. employees are often unwilling to take extensive test batteries
   B. an employer must wait until a large enough *predictive* group has been hired to
      norm the measurement
   C. *self-selection* bias can restrict the range of test scores
   D. results are often skewed toward applicants with previous experience

10. Jobs whose salaries are below the minimum of the salary range for the job are described   10.____
    as _____ jobs.

    A. broadband   B. red circle
    C. green circle   D. exempt

11. In an organization with a human resources department, which of the following informa-   11.____
    tion is most likely to be covered by the operating supervisor in orienting a new employee?

    A. A brief history of the organization
    B. Rules, regulations, policies, and procedures
    C. Personnel policies
    D. Reviewing performance criteria

12. In human resources management, *pay structure* refers to   12.____

    A. pay set relative to employees working on different jobs within the organization
    B. a grouping of a variety of work jobs that are similar in their difficulty and responsi-
       bility requirements
    C. pay set relative to employees working on similar jobs in other organizations
    D. a survey of the compensation of all employees by all employers in a geographic
       area, an industry, or an occupational group

13. Which of the following is a provision of the Rehabilitation Act, as amended?   13.____

    A. Employers may not cite the potential legal liability for drug-related injuries or acci-
       dents as a reason for firing an employee.
    B. Employers of 100 or more must establish employee assistance programs (EAPs)
       for helping drug addicts or alcoholics to recover.
    C. Employers of any size may not fire, or refuse to hire, an employee or candidate
       solely because of alcohol or drug addiction.
    D. Drug addiction and alcoholism are not be be considered *disabilities* in the same
       category as other employee handicaps.

14. A disadvantage of using ranking as a job evaluation method is that   14.____

    A. it is the slowest of all job evaluation methods
    B. it requires cumbersome descriptions of each job class
    C. it is one of the more expensive methods
    D. its results are nearly always more subjective than with other methods

15. In an organization that employs at least some union members, union members are sometimes given preferences over nonunion members in areas such as hiring, promotion, and layoff. Preferences given in this situation are often likely to violate the provisions of the _____ Act.

15.____

    A. Taft-Hartley   B. Wagner
    C. Landrum-Griffin   D. Fair Labor Standards

16. In human resources management, the _____ principle states that authority flows one link at a time, from the top of the organization to the bottom.

16.____

    A. parity   B. scalar   C. quality   D. graduation

17. When an employee training program fails, the most common reason is that

17.____

    A. training needs changed after the program had been implemented
    B. employees were not motivated
    C. there were no on-the-job rewards for behaviors and skills learned in training
    D. there were inaccurate training needs analyses

18. In implementing a progressive discipline pattern with a difficult employee, the first step is typically to

18.____

    A. issue a written warning to the employee
    B. impose a period of *decision leave* for the employee to consider his or her actions
    C. enroll the employee in additional training
    D. counsel or discuss the problem with the employee

19. The most widely used method of career planning that occurs in organizations is

19.____

    A. the planning workshop
    B. the extended seminar
    C. the self-assessment center
    D. counseling by supervisors and human resources staff

20. Under the provisions of the Equal Pay Act, differences in _____ is NOT a justification for paying a man more than a woman for the same job.

20.____

    A. performance   B. skill
    C. family situations   D. seniority

21. Compensation plans that protect the wages of workers hired before a certain date but start new workers at a lower pay rate are described as

21.____

    A. straight piecework   B. weighted
    C. two-tiered   D. differential piece rate

22. To prevent bias and legal complications, performance evaluations should steer clear of each of the following traits EXCEPT

22.____

    A. dependability   B. knowledge
    C. attitude   D. drive

23. The type of benefits most valued by employees are typically   23.____

    A. paid vacation and holidays
    B. medical
    C. long-term disability
    D. dental

24. Which of the following is the most common reason for employees to be opposed to the   24.____
process of performance evaluation?

    A. Interference with normal work patterns
    B. Operating problems
    C. Bad system design
    D. Rater subjectivity

25. _____ training is most commonly used in the workplace.   25.____

    A. Apprenticeship   B. Vestibule
    C. Cross-   D. Classroom

KEY (CORRECT ANSWERS)

1.	D		11.	D
2.	A		12.	A
3.	B		13.	B
4.	B		14.	D
5.	B		15.	A
6.	B		16.	B
7.	C		17.	C
8.	D		18.	D
9.	B		19.	D
10.	C		20.	C

21.	C
22.	B
23.	B
24.	D
25.	D

TEST 2

Each question or incomplete statement is followed by several suggested answers or completions. Select the one that BEST answers the question or completes the statement. *PRINT THE LETTER OF THE CORRECT ANSWER IN THE SPACE AT THE RIGHT.*

1. In today's personnel market, the most critical factor used by recruiters to evaluate pro-spective job candidates who hold an MBA is usually the

   A. institution from which the degree was earned
   B. applicant's interpersonal style
   C. applicant's demonstrated skill level
   D. applicant's previous work experience

   1.____

2. If a human resources manager decides to implement a preventive health care program in the workplace, he or she should be careful to guard against

   A. an increase in the number of medical claims made by employees
   B. a lack of quantifiable proof that the program is saving money or increasing produc-tivity
   C. the splintering of the wellness program into its own budgetary status
   D. the abuse of available resources by employees

   2.____

3. Competition is most likely to be a problem in performance evaluations that involve rating by

   A. the employee's subordinates
   B. the employee's peers
   C. self-evaluation
   D. a committee of several supervisors

   3.____

4. Which of the following is not a problem commonly associated with merit pay systems?

   A. Employees often fail to make the connection between pay and performance.
   B. The size of merit awards has little effect on performance.
   C. Costs are usually higher than in individual incentive plans.
   D. The secrecy of rewards is seen as inequity by employees.

   4.____

5. Which of the following step in the job analysis process is typically performed FIRST?

   A. Collecting data
   B. Selecting the jobs to be analyzed
   C. Determining how job analysis information will be used
   D. Preparing job descriptions

   5.____

6. In which of the following sectors are employees typically most expensive to train?

   A. Consumer products
   B. Agriculture/forestry/fishing
   C. Services
   D. Industrial products

   6.____

7. A commonly encountered disadvantage of using Bureau of Labor Statistics (BLS) data in pay surveys is that they

    A. tend to skew data in a way that favors labor over management
    B. are too generalized to be useful
    C. only list maximum and minimum pay rates, not medians and averages
    D. are not widely available to the public

7.____

8. Other than the salaries of training staff and trainees, which of the following is typically the largest expense involved in conducting an employee training program?

    A. Seminars and conferences
    B. Outside services
    C. Facilities and overhead
    D. Hardware

8.____

9. Under the provisions of the Equal Pay Act, differences in pay for equal work are permitted if they result from any of the following EXCEPT differences in

    A. seniority
    B. quality of performance
    C. age
    D. quantity or quality of production

9.____

10. Which of the following personnel selection procedures is typically LEAST costly?

    A. Background and reference checks
    B. Employment interview
    C. Preliminary screening
    D. Employment tests

10.____

11. Which of the following is a strictly internal method of personnel recruitment?

    A. Employment agencies
    B. Recruitment advertising
    C. Special-events recruiting
    D. Job posting

11.____

12. Of the following individual performance evaluation techniques, which has the advantage of offering the flexibility to discuss what the organization is attempting to accomplish?

    A. Graphic rating scale
    B. Behaviorally anchored rating scale (BARS)
    C. Essay evaluation
    D. Behavioral observation scale (BOS)

12.____

13. In human resources management, the *Pygmalion effect* refers to the tendency of an employee to

    A. live up to a manager's expectations
    B. identify with a working group
    C. sacrifice his or her personal life for improved work performance
    D. avoid work if at all possible

13.____

14. In medium-sized and larger organizations, the role of a human resources manager in the selection process is most often characterized by   14.____

   A. conducting the selection interview
   B. narrowing a field of applicants to a smaller, more manageable number
   C. designing the process by which candidates will be selected
   D. exercising final authority for hiring decisions

15. Employees who believe they have been discriminated against under the *whistleblowing* provisions of the Occupational Safety and Health Act may file a complaint at the nearest OSHA office within _____ of the alleged discriminatory action.   15.____

   A. 10 days   B. 30 days   C. 90 days   D. 6 months

16. Of the many applications possible with computerized human resource information systems, which of the following is most commonly used?   16.____

   A. Equal employment opportunity records
   B. Job analysis
   C. Performance appraisals
   D. Career pathing

17. _____ cost(s) is the term for expenditures for necessary items that do not become a part of a product or service.   17.____

   A. Operating supplies   B. Overhead
   C. Maintenance   D. Material

18. The union official who is responsible for representing the interests of local members in their relations with managers on the job is the   18.____

   A. president   B. business representative
   C. committee person   D. vice president

19. Of the many types of employment tests used in personnel selection, _____ tests tend to have the highest validities and reliabilities.   19.____

   A. performance simulation
   B. paper-and-pencil
   C. job sample performance
   D. personality and temperament

20. If an employee exhibits a *behavior discrepancy*—if his or her performance varies from what is expected on the job—a human resources manager might conduct a performance analysis. Most of these analyses begin with the process of   20.____

   A. motivating the employee to do better
   B. setting clear standards for performance on the job
   C. training the employee
   D. conducting a cost/value analysis of correcting the identified behavior

21. It is NOT a common goal of the orientation process to   21._____

    A. reduce personnel turnover
    C. develop realistic expectations
    B. reduce anxiety
    D. teach an employee specific job skills

22. In order for a situation to be accurately described as a job *layoff,* each of the following   22._____
conditions must occur EXCEPT

    A. there is no work available
    B. the work shortage is sudden and surprising
    C. management expects the no-work situation to be temporary
    D. management intends to recall the employee

23. In a(n) _____ payroll plan, pay is based on two separate piecework rates: one for those   23._____
who produce below or up to standard, and another for those who produce up to standard.

    A. equity
    C. functional
    B. Taylor
    D. distributive

24. Approximately what percentage of the U.S. labor force is currently unionized?   24._____

    A. 5   B. 15   C. 45   D. 70

25. The _____ principle states that managers should concentrate their efforts on matters   25._____
that deviate from the normal and let their employees handle routine matters.

    A. critical-incident   B. flow-process   C. exception   D. democratic

---

KEY (CORRECT ANSWERS)

1. B	11. D
2. B	12. C
3. B	13. A
4. C	14. B
5. C	15. B
6. D	16. A
7. B	17. A
8. C	18. C
9. C	19. C
10. C	20. D

21. D
22. B
23. B
24. B
25. C

EXAMINATION SECTION

DIRECTIONS: Each question or incomplete statement is followed by several suggested answers or completions. Select the one that BEST answers the question or completes the statement. *PRINT THE LETTER OF THE CORRECT ANSWER IN THE SPACE AT THE RIGHT.*

Questions 1-5.

DIRECTIONS: Each of Questions 1 through 5 consists of a passage which contains one word that is incorrectly used because it is not in keeping with the meaning that the quotation is evidently intended to convey. Determine which word is incorrectly used. Select from the choices lettered A, B, C, and D the word which, when substituted for the incorrectly used word, would BEST help to convey the meaning of the quotation.

1. Whatever the method, the necessity to keep up with the dynamics of an organization is the point on which many classification plans go awry. The budgetary approach to "positions," for example, often leads to using for recruitment and pay purposes a position authorized many years earlier for quite a different purpose than currently contemplated – making perhaps the title, the class, and the qualifications required inappropriate to the current need. This happens because executives overlook the stability that takes place in job duties and fail to reread an initial description of the job before saying, as they scan a list of titles, "We should fill this position right away." Once a classification plan is adopted, it is pointless to do anything less than provide for continuous, painstaking maintenance on a current basis, else once different positions that have actually become similar to each other remain in different classes, and some former cognates that have become quite different continue in the same class. Such a program often seems expensive. But to stint too much on this out-of-pocket cost may create still higher hidden costs growing out of lowered morale, poor production, delayed operating programs, excessive pay for simple work, and low pay for responsible work (resulting in poorly qualified executives and professional men) – all normal concomitants of inadequate, hasty, or out-of-date classification.   1.____

   A. evolution
   C. disapproved
   B. personnel
   D. forward

2. At first sight, it may seem that there is little or no difference between the usableness of a manual and the degree of its use. But there is a difference. A manual may have all the qualities which make up the usable manual and still not be used. Take this instance as an example: Suppose you have a satisfactory manual but issue instructions from day to day through the avenue of bulletins, memorandums, and other informational releases. Which will the employee use, the manual or the bulletin which passes over his desk? He will, of course, use the latter, for some obsolete material will not be contained in this manual. Here we have a theoretically usable manual which is unused because of the other avenues by which procedural information may be issued.   2.____

   A. countermand
   C. intentional
   B. discard
   D. worthwhile

3. By reconcentrating control over its operations in a central headquarters, a firm is able to extend the influence of automation to many, if not all, of its functions – from inventory and payroll to production, sales, and personnel. In so doing, businesses freeze all the elements of the corporate function in their relationship to one another and to the overall objectives of the firm. From this total systems concept, companies learn that computers can accomplish much more than clerical and accounting jobs. Their capabilities can be tapped to perform the traditional applications (payroll processing, inventory control, accounts payable, and accounts receivable) as well as newer applications such as spotting deviations from planned programs (exception reporting), adjusting planning schedules, forecasting business trends, simulating market conditions, and solving production problems. Since the office manager is a manager of information and each of these applications revolves around the processing of data, he must take an active role in studying and improving the system under his care.

3._____

A. maintaining B. inclusion
C. limited D. visualize

4. In addition to the formal and acceptance theories of the source of authority, although perhaps more closely related to the latter, is the belief that authority is generated by personal qualifies of technical competence. Under this heading is the individual who has made, in effect, subordinates of others through sheer force of personality, and the engineer or economist who exerts influence by furnishing answers or sound advice. These may have no actual organizational authority, yet their advice may be so eagerly sought and so unerringly followed that it appears to carry the weight of an order.
But, above all, one cannot discount the importance of formal authority with its institutional foundations. Buttressed by the qualities of leadership implicit in the acceptance theory, formal authority is basic to the managerial job. Once abrogated, it may be delegated or withheld, used or misused, and be effective in capable hands or be ineffective in inept hands.

4._____

A. selected B. delegation
C. limited D. possessed

5. Since managerial operations in organizing, staffing, directing, and controlling are designed to support the accomplishment of enterprise objectives, planning logically precedes the execution of all other managerial functions. Although all the functions intermesh in practice, planning is unique in that it establishes the objectives necessary for all group effort. Besides, plans must be made to accomplish these objectives before the manager knows what kind of organization relationships and personal qualifications are needed, along which course subordinates are to be directed, and what kind of control is to be applied. And, of course, each of the other managerial functions must be planned if they are to be effective.
Planning and control are inseparable – the Siamese twins of management. Unplanned action cannot be controlled, for control involves keeping activities on course by correcting deviations from plans. Any attempt to control without plans would be meaningless, since there is no way anyone can tell whether he is going where he wants to go – the task of control – unless first he knows where he wants to go – the task of planning. Plans thus preclude the standards of control.

5._____

A. coordinating B. individual
C. furnish D. follow

3

Questions 6-7.

DIRECTIONS: Answer Questions 6 and 7 SOLELY on the basis of information given in the following paragraph.
*In-basket tests are often used to assess managerial potential. The exercise consists of a
set of papers that would be likely to be found in the in-basket of an administrator or manager
at any given time, and requires the individuals participating in the examination to indicate how
they would dispose of each item found in the in-basket. In order to handle the in-basket effectively, they must successfully manage their time, refer and assign some work to subordinates,
juggle potentially conflicting appointments and meetings, and arrange for follow-up of problems generated by the items in the in-basket. In other words, the in-basket test is attempting
to evaluate the participants' abilities to organize their work, set priorities, delegate, control,
and make decisions.*

6.   According to the above paragraph, to succeed in an in-basket test, an administrator must   6.____

   A.   be able to read very quickly
   B.   have a great deal of technical knowledge
   C.   know when to delegate work
   D.   arrange a lot of appointments and meetings

7.   According to the above paragraph, all of the following abilities are indications of manage-   7.____
rial potential EXCEPT the ability to

   A.   organize and control   B.   manage time
   C.   write effective reports   D.   make appropriate decisions

Questions 8-9.

DIRECTIONS: Answer Questions 8 and 9 SOLELY on the basis of information given in the following paragraph.
*One of the biggest mistakes of government executives with substantial supervisory
responsibility is failing to make careful appraisals of performance during employee probationary periods. Many a later headache could have been avoided by prompt and full appraisal
during the early months of an employee's assignment. There is not much more to say about
this except to emphasize the common prevalence of this oversight, and to underscore that for
its consequences, which are many and sad, the offending managers have no one to blame
but themselves.*

8.   According to the above passage, probationary periods are   8.____

   A.   a mistake, and should not be used by supervisors with large responsibilities
   B.   not used properly by government executives
   C.   used only for those with supervisory responsibility
   D.   the consequence of management mistakes

4

9. The one of the following conclusions that can MOST appropriately be drawn from the   9.____
above passage is that

    A. management's failure to appraise employees during their probationary period is a
       common occurrence
    B. there is not much to say about probationary periods, because they are unimportant
    C. managers should blame employees for failing to use their probationary periods
       properly
    D. probationary periods are a headache to most managers

Questions 10-12.

DIRECTIONS: Answer Questions 10 through 12 SOLELY on the basis of information given in
the following paragraph.

The common sense character of the merit system seems so natural to most Americans that many people wonder why it should ever have been inoperative. After all, the American economic system, the most phenomenal the world has ever known, is also founded on a rugged selective process which emphasizes the personal qualities of capacity, industriousness, and productivity. The criteria may not have always been appropriate and competition has not always been fair, but competition there was, and the responsibilities and the rewards – with exceptions, of course – have gone to those who could measure up in terms of intelligence, knowledge, or perseverance. This has been true not only in the economic area, in the money-making process, but also in achievement in the professions and other walks of life.

10. According to the above paragraph, economic rewards in the United States have   10.____

    A. always been based on appropriate, fair criteria
    B. only recently been based on a competitive system
    C. not gone to people who compete too ruggedly
    D. usually gone to those people with intelligence, knowledge, and perseverance

11. According to the above passage, a merit system is   11.____

    A. an unfair criterion on which to base rewards
    B. unnatural to anyone who is not American
    C. based only on common sense
    D. based on the same principles as the American economic system

12. According to the above passage, it is MOST accurate to say that   12.____

    A. the United States has always had a civil service merit system
    B. civil service employees are very rugged
    C. the American economic system has always been based on a merit objective
    D. competition is unique to the American way of life

60

Questions 13-15.

DIRECTIONS: The management study of employee absence due to sickness is an effective tool in planning. Answer Questions 13 through 15 SOLELY on the data given below.

Number of days absent per worker (sickness)	1	2	3	4	5	6	7	8 or Over
Number of workers	76	23	6	3	1	0	1	0

Total Number of Workers: 400
Period Covered: January 1 - December 31

13. The total number of man days lost due to illness was   13._____

    A. 110   B. 137   C. 144   D. 164

14. What percent of the workers had 4 or more days absence due to sickness?   14._____

    A. .25%   B. 2.5%   C. 1.25%   D. 12.5%

15. Of the 400 workers studied, the number who lost no days due to sickness was   15._____

    A. 190   B. 236   C. 290   D. 346

Questions 16-18.

DIRECTIONS: In the graph below, the lines labeled "A" and "B" represent the cumulative progress in the work of two file clerks, each of whom was given 500 consecutively numbered applications to file in the proper cabinets over a five-day work week. Answer Questions 16 through 18 SOLELY upon the data provided in the graph.

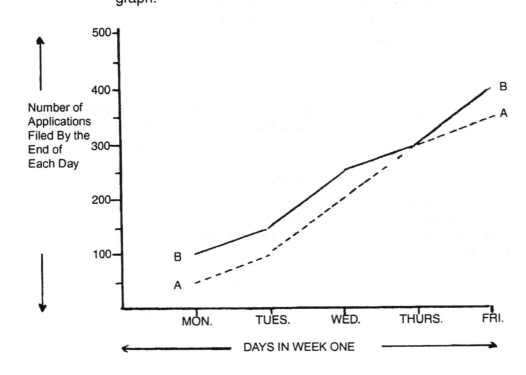

16. The day during which the LARGEST number of applications was filed by both clerks was   16._____

    A. Monday   B. Tuesday   C. Wednesday   D. Friday

17. At the end of the second day, the percentage of applications STILL to be filed was   17._____

    A. 25%   B. 50%   C. 66%   D. 75%

18. Assuming that the production pattern is the same the following week as the week shown   18._____
in the chart, the day on which the file clerks will FINISH this assignment will be

    A. Monday   B. Tuesday   C. Wednesday   D. Friday

Questions 19-21.

DIRECTIONS: The following chart shows the differences between the rates of production of employees in Department D in 1996 and 2006. Answer Questions 19 through 21 SOLELY on the basis of the information given in the chart.

Number of Employees Producing Work-Units Within Range in 1996	Number of Work-Units Produced	Number of Employees Producing Work-Units Within Range in 2006
7	500 - 1000	4
14	1001 - 1500	11
26	1501 - 2000	28
22	2001 - 2500	36
17	2501 - 3000	39
10	3001 - 3500	23
4	3501 - 4000	9

19. Assuming that within each range of work-units produced the average production was at   19._____
the mid-point at that range (e.g., category 500 - 1000 = 750), then the AVERAGE number
of work-units produced per employee in 1996 fell into the range

    A. 1001 - 1500   B. 1501 - 2000
    C. 2001 - 2500   D. 2501 - 3000

20. The ratio of the number of employees producing more than 2000 work-units in 1996 to   20._____
the number of employees producing more than 2000 work-units in 2006 is *most nearly*

    A. 1:2   B. 2:3   C. 3:4   D. 4:5

21. In Department D, which of the following were GREATER in 2006 than in 1996?   21._____
    I. Total number of employees
    II. Total number of work-units produced
    III. Number of employees producing 2000 or fewer work-units
The CORRECT answer is:

    A. I, II, III   B. I, II
    C. I, III   D. II, III

22. Unit S's production fluctuated substantially from one year to another. In 2004, Unit S's production was 100% greater than in 2003. In 2005, production decreased by 25% from 2004. In 2006, Unit S's production was 10% greater than in 2005.
On the basis of this information, it is CORRECT to conclude that Unit S's production in 2006 exceeded Unit S's production in 2003 by

    A. 65%   B. 85%   C. 95%   D. 135%

22.____

23. Agency "X" is moving into a new building. It has 1500 employees presently on its staff and does not contemplate much variance from this level. The new building contains 100 available offices, each with a maximum capacity of 30 employees. It has been decided that only 2/3 of the maximum capacity of each office will be utilized. The TOTAL number of offices that will be occupied by Agency "X" is

    A. 30   B. 66   C. 75   D. 90

23.____

24. One typist completes a form letter every 5 minutes and another typist completes one every 6 minutes.
If the two typists start together, they will again start typing new letters simultaneously _____ minutes later and will have completed _____ letters by that time.

    A. 11; 30   B. 12; 24   C. 24; 12   D. 30; 11

24.____

25. During one week, a machine operator produces 10 fewer pages per hour of work than he usually does. If it ordinarily takes him six hours to produce a 300-page report, it will take him____hours LONGER to produce that same 300-page report during the week when he produces MORE slowly.

    A. $1\frac{1}{2}$ B. $1\frac{2}{3}$ C. 2   D. $2\frac{3}{4}$

25.____

——————

KEY (CORRECT ANSWERS)

Incorrect Words

1.	A	stability
2.	D	obsolete
3.	D	freeze
4.	D	abrogated
5.	C	preclude

6.	C	16.	C
7.	C	17.	D
8.	B	18.	B
9.	A	19.	C
10.	D	20.	A
11.	D	21.	B
12.	C	22.	A
13.	D	23.	C
14.	C	24.	D
15.	C	25.	A

EXAMINATION SECTION
TEST 1

DIRECTIONS: Each question or incomplete statement is followed by several suggested answers or completions. Select the one that BEST answers the question or completes the statement. *PRINT THE LETTER OF THE CORRECT ANSWER IN THE SPACE AT THE RIGHT.*

1. Assume that a civil service list has been established for a position in an agency which had provisional appointees serving in three permanent vacancies. One of these provisionals is on the eligible list, but was discharged because permanent appointments were accepted by three eligibles who were higher on the list. The former provisional has complained to the agency head, alleging that special efforts were made to appoint these eligibles. The personnel officer of the agency should advise the agency head that

    A. the court could compel him to appoint the former provisional appointee
    B. he is required by civil service law to appoint the higher ranking eligibles from the list
    C. the human rights commission could compel him to appoint the former provisional appointee
    D. he should attempt conciliation

1.____

2. Assume that two accountants working in a section under your supervision were appointed from the same eligible list. Accountant Jones received a higher score on the competitive examination than Accountant Doe; Jones was third on the eligible list and Doe was fifth. Jones was told to report to work on March 15 but Doe, who was working under a provisional appointment, was given permanent status as of March 1. For economy reasons, your agency head is considering abolishing one position of accountant and requests guidance from you before making any decision.
It would be BEST to tell him that

    A. if he decides to abolish one position of accountant, he should lay off Jones because Doe was given permanent status before Jones
    B. under the rule of *one in three* Doe could not have been reached for appointment before Jones, so that Doe would have to be laid off first
    C. if he decides to abolish one position of accountant, he should lay off Doe because Doe's provisional appointment was in violation of the Civil Service Law
    D. he should evaluate the performance of Jones and Doe before making any determination as to which accountant to lay off

2.____

3. An employee who has been on the job for a number of years became a problem drinker during the past year. The supervisor and this employee are good friends.
Because this problem has been affecting the work of the unit adversely, it would be BEST for the supervisor to

    A. attempt to cover up the problem by moving the subordinate's desk to a corner of the office where he would not be noticed so readily
    B. refer the employee for counseling to the employee counseling service
    C. reassign some of the problem drinker's responsibilities to other employees
    D. send the employee home in a tactful manner whenever he reports for duty in an unfit condition

3.____

4. In a strike situation, a member of the striking union reports for work but abstains from the full performance of his duties in his normal manner.
   According to the state civil service law, it is *accurate* to say that the

   A. employee should be presumed to have engaged in a strike
   B. employee should not be presumed to have engaged in a strike
   C. city must bear the burden of proving that the employee engaged in a strike
   D. city may deny the employee the opportunity to rebut any charge that he engaged in a strike

4.____

5. Assume that, as a manager in a health agency which is establishing a *management-by-objectives* program, you are asked to review and make recommendations on the following goals set by the agency head for the coming year.
   Which one of these objectives should you recommend dropping because of difficulty in verifying the degree to which the goal has been attained?

   A. Establishing night clinics in two preventive health care centers
   B. Informing more people of available health services
   C. Preparing a training manual for data-processing personnel
   D. Producing a 4-page health news bulletin to be distributed monthly to employees

5.____

6. The MAIN purpose of the *management-by-objectives* system is to

   A. develop a method of appraising the performance of managerial employees against verifiable objectives rather than against subjective appraisals and personal supervision
   B. decentralize managerial decision-making more effectively by setting goals for personnel all the way down to each first-line supervisor as well as to staff people
   C. increase managerial accountability and improve managerial effectiveness
   D. enable top level managerial employees to impose quantitative goals which will focus attention on the relevant trends that may affect the future

6.____

7. Certain city and state employees are on one year's probation for violating the strike provisions of the state civil service law.
   According to a ruling by the state attorney general, in the event of layoffs during their year of probation, the status of these employees should be considered

   A. *permanent,* with retention rights based on original date of appointment
   B. *probationary,* subject to layoff before permanent employees
   C. *permanent,* to be credited with one year less service than indicated by the original date of appointment
   D. *probationary,* subject to layoff before other employees in the layoff unit except for those with one year's seniority

7.____

8. Assume that, as a senior supervisor conducting a training course for a group of newly-assigned first-line supervisors, you emphasize that an effective supervisor should encourage employee suggestions. One member of the group dissents, asserting that many employees come up with worthless, time-wasting ideas.
   The one of the following which would be the MOST appropriate response for you to make is that

8.____

A.   the supervisor's attitude is wrong, because no suggestion is entirely without merit
B.   the supervisor must remember that encouragement of employee suggestions is the major part of any employee development program
C.   even if a suggestion seems worthless, the participation of the employee helps to increase his identification with the agency
D.   even if a suggestion seems worthless, the supervisor may be able to save it for future use

9.   The *grapevine* is an informal channel of communication which exists among employees in an organization as a natural result of their social interaction, and their desire to be kept posted on the latest information. Some information transmitted through the grapevine is truth, some half-truth, and some just rumor.
Which one of the following would be the MOST appropriate attitude for a member of a management team to have about the grapevine?

    9.____

A.   The grapevine often carries false, malicious, and uncontrollable rumors and management should try to stamp it out by improving official channels of communication.
B.   There are more important problems; normally only a small percentage of employees are interested in information transmitted through the grapevine.
C.   The grapevine can give management insight into what employees think and feel and can help to supplement the formal communication systems.
D.   The grapevine gives employees a harmless outlet for their imagination and an opportunity to relieve their fears and tensions in the form of rumors.

10.   Although there are no formal performance appraisal mechanisms for non-managerial employees, managers nevertheless make informal appraisals because some method is needed to measure progress and to let employees know how they are doing.
The MOST important recent trend in making performance appraisals is toward judging the employee *primarily* on the extent to which he has

    10.____

A.   tried to perform his assigned tasks
B.   demonstrated personal traits which are accepted as necessary to do the job satisfactorily
C.   accomplished the objectives set for his job
D.   followed the procedures established for the job

11.   The proof of a successful human relations program in an organization is the morale crises that never happen.
Of the following, the implication for managers that follows MOST directly from this statement is that they should

    11.____

A.   review and initiate revisions in all organization policies which may have an adverse effect on employee morale
B.   place more emphasis on ability to anticipate and prevent morale problems than on ability to resolve an actual crisis
C.   see that first-line supervisors work fairly and understandingly with employees
D.   avoid morale crises at all costs, since even the best resolution leaves scars, suspicions, and animosities

12. Suppose that you are conducting a conference on a specific problem. One employee   12.____
    makes a suggestion which you think is highly impractical.
    Of the following, the way for you to respond to this suggestion is FIRST to

    A. be frank and tell the employee that his solution is wrong
    B. ask the employee in what way his suggestion will solve the problem under discus-
       sion
    C. refrain from any comment on it, and ask the group whether they have any other
       solutions to offer
    D. ask another participant to point out what is wrong with the suggestion

13. Suppose that a manager notices continuing deterioration in the work, conduct, and inter-   13.____
    personal relationships of one of his immediate subordinates, indicating that this
    employee has more than a minor emotional problem. Although the manager has made
    an attempt to help this employee by talking over his problems with him on several occa-
    sions, the employee has shown little improvement.
    Of the following, generally the MOST constructive action for the manager to take at
    this point would be to

    A. continue to be supportive by sympathetic listening and counseling
    B. show tolerance toward the performance of the disturbed employee
    C. discuss the employee's deteriorating condition with him and suggest that he seek
       professional help
    D. consider whether the needs of this employee and the agency would be best served
       by his transfer to another division

14. A manager has a problem involving conflict between two employees concerning a   14.____
    method of performing a work assignment. He does not know the reasons for this conflict.
    The MOST valuable communications method he can use to aid him in resolving the
    problem is

    A. a formal hearing for each employee
    B. a staff meeting
    C. disciplinary memoranda
    D. an informal interview with each employee

15. As a training technique, role-playing is generally considered to be MOST successful   15.____
    when it results in

    A. uncovering the underlying causes of conflict so that any recurrences are prevented
    B. recreating an actual work situation which involves conflict among people and in
       which members of the group simulate specific personalities
    C. freeing people from patterns of rigid thinking and enabling them to look at them-
       selves and others in a new way
    D. increasing the participants' powers of logic and reasoning

16. In conducting a disciplinary interview, a supervisor finds that he must ask some highly   16.____
    personal questions which are relevant to the problem at hand.
    The interviewer is MOST likely to get *truthful* answers to these questions if he asks
    them

A. early in the interview, before the interviewee has had a chance to become emotional

B. in a manner so that the interviewee can answer them with a simple *yes* or *no*

C. well into the interview, after rapport and trust have been established

D. just after the close of the interview, so that the questions appear to be off the record

17. Suppose that, as a newly assigned manager, you observe that a supervisor in your division uses autocratic methods which are causing resentment among his subordinates. Of the following, the MOST likely reason for this supervisor's using such methods is that he   17._____

A. was probably exposed to this type of supervision himself

B. does not have an intuitive sense of tact, diplomacy, and consideration and no amount of training can change this

C. received approval for use of such methods from his former subordinates

D. does not understand the basic concept of rewards and punishments in the practice of supervision

18. A newly appointed employee, Mr. Jones, was added to the staff of a supervisor who, because of the pressure of other work, turned him over to an experienced subordinate by saying, *Show Mr. Jones around and give him something to do.*
On the basis of this experience, Mr. Jones' FIRST impression of his new position was most likely to have been   18._____

A. *negative,* mainly because it appeared that his job was not worth his supervisor's attention

B. *negative,* mainly because the more experienced subordinate would tend to emphasize the unpleasant aspects of the work

C. *positive,* mainly because his supervisor wasted no time in assigning him to a subordinate

D. *positive,* mainly because he saw himself working for a dynamic supervisor who expected immediate results

19. An employee who stays in one assignment for a number of years often develops a feeling of possessiveness concerning his knowledge of the job which may develop into a problem.
Of the following, the BEST way for a supervisor to remedy this difficulty is to   19._____

A. give the employee less important work to do

B. point out minor errors as often as possible

C. raise performance standards for all employees

D. rotate the employee to a different assignment

20. A supervisor who tends to be supportive of his subordinates, in contrast to a supervisor who relies upon an authoritarian style of leadership, is more likely, in dealing with his staff, to have to listen to complaints, to have to tolerate emotionally upset employees, and even have to hear unreasonable and insulting remarks.
Compared to the authoritarian supervisor, he is MORE likely to   20._____

A. be unconsciously fearful of failure

B. have an overriding interest in production

C. have subordinates who are better educated

D. receive accurate feedback information

69

KEY (CORRECT ANSWERS)

1.	B	11.	B
2.	B	12.	B
3.	B	13.	C
4.	A	14.	D
5.	B	15.	C
6.	C	16.	C
7.	B	17.	A
8.	C	18.	A
9.	C	19.	D
10.	C	20.	D

TEST 2

DIRECTIONS: Each question or incomplete statement is followed by several suggested answers or completions. Select the one that BEST answers the question or completes the statement. *PRINT THE LETTER OF THE CORRECT ANSWER IN THE SPACE AT THE RIGHT.*

1. Assume that one of your subordinates, a supervisor in charge of a small unit in your 1.____ bureau, asks your advice in handling a situation which has just occurred in his unit. On returning from a meeting the supervisor notices that Jane Jones, the unit secretary, is not at her regular work location. Another employee had become faint, and the secretary accompanied this employee outdoors for some fresh air. It is a long-standing rule that no employee is permitted to leave the building during office hours except on official busi-ness or with the unit head's approval. Quite recently another employee was reprimanded by the supervisor for going out at 10 A.M. for a cup of coffee.
Of the following, it would be BEST for you to advise the supervisor to

   A. circulate a memo within the unit, restating the department's regulation concerning leaving the building during office hours
   B. overlook this rule violation in view of the extenuating circumstances
   C. personally reprimand the unit secretary since all employees must be treated in the same way when official rules are broken
   D. tell the unit secretary that you should reprimand her, but that you've decided to overlook the rule infraction this time

2. Of the following, the MOST valid reason why the application of behavioral modification 2.____ techniques to management of large organizations is not yet widely accepted by manag-ers is that these techniques are

   A. based mainly on research conducted under highly controlled conditions
   B. more readily adaptable to training unskilled employees
   C. incompatible with the validated *management-by-objectives* approach
   D. manipulative and incompatible with the democratic approach

3. Because of intensive pressures which have developed since the onset of the city's finan- 3.____ cial problems, the members of a certain bureau have begun to file grievances about their working conditions. These protests are accumulating at a much greater rate than normal and faster than they can be disposed of under the current state of affairs. Concerned about the possible effect of these unresolved matters on the productivity of the bureau at such a critical time, the administrator in charge decides to take immediate action to improve staff relationships. With this intention in mind, he should

   A. explain to the staff why their grievances cannot be handled at the present time; then inform them that there will be a moratorium on the filing of additional griev-ances until the current backlog has been eliminated
   B. assemble all grievants at a special meeting and assure them that their problems will be handled in due course, but the current pressures preclude the prompt set-tling of their grievances

    C.   assign the assistant directors of the bureau to immediately schedule and conduct hearings on the accumulated grievances until the backlog is eliminated

    D.   suggest that the grievants again confer with their supervisors about their problems, orally rather than in writing, with direct appeal to him for such cases as are not resolved in this manner

4.   A supervisor is attending a staff meeting with other accounting supervisors during which the participants are to propose various possible methods of dealing with a complex operational problem.   4.____
The one of the following procedures which will MOST likely produce an acceptable proposal for solving this problem at this meeting is for the

    A.   group to agree at the beginning of the meeting on the kinds of approaches to the problem that are most likely to succeed

    B.   conference leader to set a firm time limit on the period during which the participants are to present whatever ideas come to mind

    C.   group to discuss each proposal fully before the next proposal is made

    D.   conference leader to urge every participant in the meeting to present at least one proposal

5.   Which one of the following types of communication systems would foster an authoritarian atmosphere in a large agency?   5.____
A communication system which

    A.   is restricted to organizational procedures and specific job instructions

    B.   provides information to employees about the rationale for their jobs

    C.   informs employees about their job performance

    D.   provides information about the relationship of employees' work to the agency's goals

6.   According to most management experts, the one of the following which would generally have SERIOUS shortcomings as a component of a performance evaluation program is   6.____

    A.   rating the performance of each subordinate against the performance of other subordinates

    B.   limiting the appraisal to an evaluation of current performance

    C.   rating each subordinate in terms of clearly stated, measurable job goals

    D.   interviewing the subordinate to discuss present job performance and ways of improvement

7.   Which of the following is consistent with the management-by-objectives approach as used in a fiscal affairs division of a large city agency?   7.____

    A.   Performance goals for the division are established by the administrator, who requires daily progress reports for each accounting unit.

    B.   Each subordinate accountant participates in setting his own short term performance goals.

    C.   A detailed set of short-term performance goals for each accountant is prepared by his supervisor.

    D.   Objectives are established and progress evaluated by a committee of administrative accountants.

Questions 8-11.

DIRECTIONS: Questions 8 through 11 are to be answered on the basis of the information
given below.

Assume that you are the director of a small bureau, organized into three divisions. The bureau has a total of twenty employees: fourteen in professional titles and six in clerical titles. Each division has a chief who reports directly to you and who supervises five employees.

For Questions 8 through 11, you are to select the MOST appropriate training method, from the four choices given, based on the situation in the question:
  A.   Lecture, with a small blackboard available
  B.   Lecture, with audio-visual aids
  C.   Conference
  D.   Buddy system (experienced worker is accompanied by worker to be trained)

8.   A major reorganization of your department was completed. You have decided to conduct   8._____
a training session of about one hour's duration for all your subordinates in order to
acquaint them with the new departmental structure as well as the new responsibilities
which have been assigned to the divisions of your bureau.

9.   Three assistant supervisors, each with one year of service in your department, are trans-   9._____
ferred to your bureau as part of the process of strengthening the major activity of your
bureau. In connection with their duties, they are required to do field visits to business
firms located in the various industrial areas of the city.

10.   The work of your bureau requires that various forms be processed sequentially through   10._____
each of three divisions. In recent weeks, you have received complaints from the division
chiefs that their production is being impeded by a lack of cooperation from the chiefs and
workers in the other divisions.

11.   In order to improve the efficiency of the department, your department head has directed   11._____
that all bureaus hold weekly, thirty-minute-long training sessions for all employees, to
review relevant work procedures.

12.   Which one of the following actions is usually MOST appropriate for a manager to take in   12._____
order to encourage and develop coordination of effort among different units or individuals
within an organization?

  A.   Providing rewards to the most productive employees
  B.   Giving employees greater responsibility and the authority to exercise it
  C.   Emphasizing to the employees that it is important to coordinate their efforts
  D.   Explaining the goals of the organization to the employees and how their jobs relate
to those goals

13.   The management of time is one of the critical aspects of any supervisor's performance.   13._____
Therefore, in evaluating a subordinate from the viewpoint of how he manages time, a
supervisor should rate HIGHEST the subordinate who

A. concentrates on each task as he undertakes it
B. performs at a standard and predictable pace under all circumstances
C. takes shortened lunch periods when he is busy
D. tries to do two things simultaneously

14. A MAJOR research finding regarding employee absenteeism is that   14._____

A. absenteeism is likely to be higher on hot days
B. male employees tend to be absent more than female employees
C. the way an employee is treated has a definite bearing on absenteeism
D. the distance employees have to travel is one of the most important factors in absenteeism

15. Of the following, the supervisory behavior that is of GREATEST benefit to the organiza-   15._____
tion is exhibited by supervisors who

A. are strict with subordinates about following rules and regulations
B. encourage subordinates to be interested in the work
C. are willing to assist with subordinates' work on most occasions
D. get the most done with available staff and resources

16. In order to maintain a proper relationship with a worker who is assigned to staff rather   16._____
than line functions, a line supervisor should

A. accept all recommendations of the staff worker
B. include the staff worker in the conferences called by the supervisor for his subordi-
nates
C. keep the staff worker informed of developments in the area of his staff assignment
D. require that the staff worker's recommendations be communicated to the supervi-
sor through the supervisor's own superior

17. Of the following, the GREATEST disadvantage of placing a worker in a staff position   17._____
under the direct supervision of the supervisor whom he advises is the possibility that the

A. staff worker will tend to be insubordinate because of a feeling of superiority over
the supervisor
B. staff worker will tend to give advice of the type which the supervisor wants to hear
or finds acceptable
C. supervisor will tend to be mistrustful of the advice of a worker of subordinate rank
D. supervisor will tend to derive little benefit from the advice because to supervise
properly he should know at least as much as his subordinate

18. One factor which might be given consideration in deciding upon the optimum span of   18._____
control of a supervisor over his immediate subordinates is the position of the supervisor
in the hierarchy of the organization. It is generally considered proper that the number of
subordinates immediately supervised by a higher, upper echelon, supervisor

A. is unrelated to and tends to form no pattern with the number supervised by lower
level supervisors
B. should be about the same as the number supervised by a lower level supervisor
C. should be larger than the number supervised by a lower level supervisor
D. should be smaller than the number supervised by a lower level supervisor

19. Assume that you are a supervisor and have been assigned to assist the head of a large agency unit. He asks you to prepare a simple, functional organization chart of the unit. Such a chart would be USEFUL for

    A. favorably impressing members of the public with the important nature of the agency's work
    B. graphically presenting staff relationships which may indicate previously unknown duplications, overlaps, and gaps in job duties
    C. motivating all employees toward better performance because they will have a better understanding of job procedures
    D. subtly and inoffensively making known to the staff in the unit that you are now in a position of responsibility

19.____

20. In some large organizations, management's traditional means of learning about employee dissatisfaction has been the *open door policy*.
This policy *usually* means that

    A. management lets it be known that a management representative is generally available to discuss employees' questions, suggestions, and complaints
    B. management sets up an informal employee organization to establish a democratic procedure for orderly representation of employees
    C. employees are encouraged to attempt to resolve dissatisfactions at the lowest possible level of authority
    D. employees are provided with an address or box so that they may safely and anonymously register complaints

20.____

KEY (CORRECT ANSWERS)

1.	B	11.	A
2.	A	12.	D
3.	D	13.	A
4.	B	14.	C
5.	A	15.	D
6.	A	16.	C
7.	B	17.	B
8.	B	18.	D
9.	D	19.	B
10.	C	20.	A

READING COMPREHENSION
UNDERSTANDING AND INTERPRETING WRITTEN MATERIAL
EXAMINATION SECTION
TEST 1

DIRECTIONS: Each question or incomplete statement is followed by several suggested answers or completions. Select the one that BEST answers the question or completes the statement. *PRINT THE LETTER OF THE CORRECT ANSWER IN THE SPACE AT THE RIGHT.*

Questions 1-2.

DIRECTIONS: Questions 1 and 2 are to be answered SOLELY on the basis of the following passage.

The employees in a unit or division of a government agency may be referred to as a work group. Within a government agency which has existed for some time, the work groups will have evolved traditions of their own. The persons in these work groups acquire these traditions as part of the process of work adjustment within their groups. Usually, a work group in a large organization will contain *oldtimers*, *newcomers*, and *in-betweeners*. Like the supervisor of a group, who is not necessarily an oldtimer or the oldest member, oldtimers usually have great influence. They can recall events unknown to others and are a storehouse of information and advice about current problems in the light of past experience. They pass along the traditions of the group to the others who, in turn, become oldtimers themselves. Thus, the traditions of the group which have been honored and revered by long acceptance are continued.

1.   According to the above passage, the traditions of a work group within a government agency are developed

    A.   at the time the group is established
    B.   over a considerable period of time
    C.   in order to give recognition to oldtimers
    D.   for the group before it is established

1.____

2.   According to the above passage, the oldtimers within a work group

    A.   are the means by which long accepted practices and customs are perpetuated
    B.   would best be able to settle current problems that arise
    C.   are honored because of the changes they have made in the traditions
    D.   have demonstrated that they have learned to do their work well

2.____

Questions 3-4.

DIRECTIONS: Questions 3 and 4 are to be answered SOLELY on the basis of the following passage.

In public agencies, the success of a person assigned to perform first-line supervisory duties depends in large part upon the personal relations between him and his subordinate employees. The goal of supervising effort is something more than to obtain compliance with procedures established by some central office. The major objective is work accomplishment. In order for this goal to be attained, employees must want to attain it and must exercise initiative in their work. Only if employees are generally satisfied with the type of supervision which exists in an organization will they put forth their best efforts.

3. According to the above passage, in order for employees to try to do their work as well as they can, it is essential that   3.___

   A.   they participate in determining their working conditions and rates of pay
   B.   their supervisors support the employees' viewpoints in meetings with higher management
   C.   they are content with the supervisory practices which are being used
   D.   their supervisors make the changes in working procedures that the employees request

4. It can be inferred from the above passage that the goals of a unit in a public agency will not be reached unless the employees in the unit   4.___

   A.   wish to reach them and are given the opportunity to make individual contributions to the work
   B.   understand the relationship between the goals of the unit and goals of the agency
   C.   have satisfactory personal relationships with employees of other units in the agency
   D.   carefully follow the directions issued by higher authorities

Questions 5-9.

DIRECTIONS: Questions 5 through 9 are to be answered SOLELY on the basis of the following passage.

If an employee thinks he can save money, time, or material for the city or has an idea about how to do something better than it is being done, he shouldn't keep it to himself. He should send his ideas to the Employees' Suggestion Program, using the special form which is kept on hand in all departments. An employee may send in as many ideas as he wishes. To make sure that each idea is judged fairly, the name of the suggester is not made known until an award is made. The awards are certificates of merit or cash prizes ranging from $10 to $500.

5. According to the above passage, an employee who knows how to do a job in a better way should   5.___

   A.   be sure it saves enough time to be worthwhile
   B.   get paid the money he saves for the city
   C.   keep it to himself to avoid being accused of causing a speed-up
   D.   send his idea to the Employees' Suggestion Program

6. In order to send his idea to the Employees' Suggestion Program, an employee should   6._____

    A. ask the Department of Personnel for a special form
    B. get the special form in his own department
    C. mail the idea using Special Delivery
    D. send it on plain, white letter-size paper

7. An employee may send to the Employees' Suggestion Program   7._____

    A. as many ideas as he can think of
    B. no more than one idea each week
    C. no more than ten ideas in a month
    D. only one idea on each part of the job

8. The reason the name of an employee who makes a suggestion is not made known at first is to   8._____

    A. give the employee a larger award
    B. help the judges give more awards
    C. insure fairness in judging
    D. only one idea on each part of the job

9. An employee whose suggestion receives an award may be given a   9._____

    A. bonus once a year   B. certificate for $10
    C. cash prize of up to $500   D. salary increase of $500

Questions 10-12.

DIRECTIONS: Questions 10 through 12 are to be answered SOLELY on the basis of the following passage.

According to the rules of the Department of Personnel, the work of every permanent city employee is reviewed and rated by his supervisor at least once a year. The civil service rating system gives the employee and his supervisor a chance to talk about the progress made during the past year as well as about those parts of the job in which the employee needs to do better. In order to receive a pay increase each year, the employee must have a satisfactory service rating. Service ratings also count toward an employee's final mark on a promotion examination.

10. According to the above passage, a permanent city employee is rated AT LEAST once   10._____

    A. before his work is reviewed
    B. every six months
    C. yearly by his supervisor
    D. yearly by the Department of Personnel

11. According to the above passage, under the rating system the supervisor and the employee can discuss how   11._____

    A. much more work needs to be done next year
    B. the employee did his work last year

C. the work can be made easier next year
D. the work of the Department can be increased

12. According to the above passage, a permanent city employee will NOT receive a yearly   12.____
    pay increase

    A. if he received a pay increase the year before
    B. if he used his service rating for his mark on a promotion examination
    C. if his service rating is unsatisfactory
    D. unless he got some kind of a service rating

Questions 13-16.

DIRECTIONS: Questions 13 through 16 are to be answered SOLELY on the basis of the
            following passage.

It is an accepted fact that the rank and file employee can frequently advance worthwhile
suggestions toward increasing efficiency. For this reason, an Employees' Suggestion System
has been developed and put into operation. Suitable means have been provided at each
departmental location for the confidential submission of suggestions. Numerous suggestions
have been received thus far and, after study, about five percent of the ideas submitted are
being translated into action. It is planned to set up, eventually, monetary awards for all worthwhile suggestions.

13. According to the above passage, a MAJOR reason why an Employees' Suggestion Sys-   13.____
    tem was established is that

    A. an organized program of improvement is better than a haphazard one
    B. employees can often give good suggestions to increase efficiency
    C. once a fact is accepted, it is better to act on it than to do nothing
    D. the suggestions of rank and file employees were being neglected

14. According to the above passage, under the Employees' Suggestion System,   14.____

    A. a file of worthwhile suggestions will eventually be set up at each departmental
        location
    B. it is possible for employees to turn in suggestions without fellow employees know-
        ing of it
    C. means have been provided for the regular and frequent collection of suggestions
        submitted
    D. provision has been made for the judging of worthwhile suggestions by an Employ-
        ees' Suggestion Committee

15. According to the above passage, it is reasonable to assume that   15.____

    A. all suggestions must be turned in at a central office
    B. employees who make worthwhile suggestions will be promoted
    C. not all the prizes offered will be monetary ones
    D. prizes of money will be given for the best suggestions

16. According to the above passage, of the many suggestions made,　　　　16.____

    A. all are first tested
    B. a small part are put into use
    C. most are very worthwhile
    D. samples are studied

Questions 17-20.

DIRECTIONS:　Questions 17 through 20 are to be answered SOLELY on the basis of the following passage.

Employees may be granted leaves of absence without pay at the discretion of the Personnel Officer. Such a leave without pay shall begin on the first working day on which the employee does not report for duty and shall continue to the first day on which the employee returns to duty. The Personnel Division may vary the dates of the leave for the record so as to conform with payroll periods, but in no case shall an employee be off the payroll for a different number of calendar days than would have been the case if the actual dates mentioned above had been used. An employee who has vacation or overtime to his credit, which is available for normal use, may take time off immediately prior to beginning a leave of absence without pay, chargeable against all or part of such vacation or overtime.

17. According to the above passage, the Personnel Officer must　　　　17.____

    A. decide if a leave of absence without pay should be granted
    B. require that a leave end on the last working day of a payroll period
    C. see to it that a leave of absence begins on the first working day of a pay period
    D. vary the dates of a leave of absence to conform with a payroll period

18. According to the above passage, the exact dates of a leave of absence without pay may be varied provided that the　　　　18.____

    A. calendar days an employee is off the payroll equal the actual leave granted
    B. leave conforms to an even number of payroll periods
    C. leave when granted made provision for variance to simplify payroll records
    D. Personnel Officer approves the variation

19. According to the above passage, a leave of absence without pay must extend from the　　　　19.____

    A. first day of a calendar period to the first day the employee resumes work
    B. first day of a payroll period to the last calendar day of the leave
    C. first working day missed to the first day on which the employee resumes work
    D. last day on which an employee works through the first day he returns to work

20. According to the above passage, an employee may take extra time off just before the start of a leave of absence without pay if　　　　20.____

    A. he charges this extra time against his leave
    B. he has a favorable balance of vacation or overtime which has been frozen
    C. the vacation or overtime that he would normally use for a leave without pay has not been charged in this way before
    D. there is time to his credit which he may use

Question 21.

DIRECTIONS: Question 21 is to be answered SOLELY on the basis of the following passage.

In considering those things which are motivators and incentives to work, it might be just as erroneous not to give sufficient weight to money as an incentive as it is to give too much weight. It is not a problem of establishing a rank-order of importance, but one of knowing that motivation is a blend or mixture rather than a pure element. It is simple to say that cultural factors count more than financial considerations, but this leads only to the conclusion that our society is financial-oriented.

21.   Based on the above passage, in our society, cultural and social motivations to work are   21.____

    A.   things which cannot be avoided
    B.   melded to financial incentives
    C.   of less consideration than high pay
    D.   not balanced equally with economic or financial considerations

Question 22.

DIRECTIONS: Question 22 is to be answered SOLELY on the basis of the following passage.

A general principle of training and learning with respect to people is that they learn more readily if they receive *feedback.* Essential to maintaining proper motivational levels is knowledge of results which indicate level of progress. Feedback also assists the learning process by identifying mistakes. If this kind of information were not given to the learner, then improper or inappropriate job performance may be instilled.

22.   Based on the above passage, which of the following is MOST accurate?   22.____

    A.   Learning will not take place without feedback.
    B.   In the absence of feedback, improper or inappropriate job performance will be learned.
    C.   To properly motivate a learner, the learner must have his progress made known to him.
    D.   Trainees should be told exactly what to do if they are to learn properly.

Question 23.

DIRECTIONS: Question 23 is to be answered SOLELY on the basis of the following passage.

In a democracy, the obligation of public officials is twofold. They must not only do an efficient and satisfactory job of administration, but also they must persuade the public that it is an efficient and satisfactory job. It is a burden which, if properly assumed, will make democracy work and perpetuate reform government.

23.   The above passage means that   23.____

    A.   public officials should try to please everybody
    B.   public opinion is instrumental in determining the policy of public officials

C. satisfactory performance of the job of administration will eliminate opposition to its work
D. frank and open procedure in a public agency will aid in maintaining progressive government

Question 24.

DIRECTIONS: Question 24 is to be answered SOLELY on the basis of the following passage.

Upon retirement for service, a member shall receive a retirement allowance which shall consist of an annuity which shall be the actuarial equivalent of his accumulated deductions at the time of his retirement and a pension, in addition to his annuity, which shall be equal to one service-fraction of his final compensation, multiplied by the number of years of service since he last became a member credited to him, and a pension which is the actuarial equivalent of the reserve-for-increased-take-home-pay to which he may then be entitled, if any.

24. According to the above passage, a retirement allowance shall consist of a(n)   24._____

A. annuity, plus a pension, plus an actuarial equivalent
B. annuity, plus a pension, plus reserve-for-increased-take-home-pay, if any
C. annuity, plus reserve-for-increased-take-home-pay, if any, plus final compensation
D. pension, plus reserve-for-increased-take-home-pay, if any, plus accumulated deductions

Question 25.

DIRECTIONS: Question 25 is to be answered SOLELY on the basis of the following passage.

Membership in the retirement system shall cease upon the occurrence of any one of the following conditions: when the time out of service of any member who has total service of less than 25 years, shall aggregate more than 5 years; when the time out of service of any member who has total service of 25 years or more, shall aggregate more than 10 years; when any member shall have withdrawn more than 50% of his accumulated deductions; or when any member shall have withdrawn the cash benefit provided by Section B3-35.0 of the Administrative Code.

25. According to the information in the above passage, membership in the retirement system   25._____
shall cease when an employee

A. with 17 years of service has been on a leave of absence for 3 years
B. withdraws 50% of his accumulated deductions
C. with 28 years of service has been out of service for 10 years
D. withdraws his cash benefits

KEY (CORRECT ANSWERS)

1.	B		11.	B
2.	A		12.	C
3.	C		13.	B
4.	A		14.	B
5.	D		15.	D
6.	B		16.	B
7.	A		17.	A
8.	C		18.	A
9.	B		19.	C
10.	C		20.	D

21.	B
22.	C
23.	D
24.	B
25.	D

TEST 2

DIRECTIONS: Each question or incomplete statement is followed by several suggested answers or completions. Select the one that BEST answers the question or completes the statement. *PRINT THE LETTER OF THE CORRECT ANSWER IN THE SPACE AT THE RIGHT.*

Questions 1-6.

DIRECTIONS: Questions 1 through 6 are to be answered SOLELY on the basis of the following passage from an old office manual.

Since almost every office has some contact with data-processed records, a stenographer should have some understanding of the basic operations of data processing. Data processing systems now handle about one-third of all office paperwork. On punched cards, magnetic tape, or on other mediums, data are recorded before being fed into the computer for processing. A machine such as the keypunch is used to convert the data written on the source document into the coded symbols on punched cards or tapes. After data has been converted, it must be verified to guarantee absolute accuracy of conversion. In this manner, data becomes a permanent record which can be read by electronic computers that compare, store, compute, and otherwise process data at high speeds.

One key person in a computer installation is a programmer, the man or woman who puts business and scientific problems into special symbolic languages that can be read by the computer. Jobs done by the computer range all the way from payroll operations to chemical process control, but most computer applications are directed toward management data. About half of the programmers employed by business come to their positions with college degrees; the remaining half are promoted to their positions from within the organization on the basis of demonstrated ability without regard to education.

1. Of the following, the BEST title for the above passage is   1.____

    A. THE STENOGRAPHER AS DATA PROCESSOR
    B. THE RELATION OF KEYPUNCHING TO STENOGRAPHY
    C. UNDERSTANDING DATA PROCESSING
    D. PERMANENT OFFICE RECORDS

2. According to the above passage, a stenographer should understand the basic operations of data processing because   2.____

    A. almost every office today has contact with data processed by computer
    B. any office worker may be asked to verify the accuracy of data
    C. most offices are involved in the production of permanent records
    D. data may be converted into computer language by typing on a keypunch

3. According to the above passage, the data which the computer understands is MOST often expressed as   3.____

    A. a scientific programming language
    B. records or symbols punched on tape, cards, or other mediums
    C. records on cards
    D. records on tape

4. According to the above passage, computers are used MOST often to handle   4._____

    A. management data
    B. problems of higher education
    C. the control of chemical processes
    D. payroll operations

5. Computer programming is taught in many colleges and business schools.   5._____
    The above passage implies that programmers in industry

    A. must have professional training
    B. need professional training to advance
    C. must have at least a college education to do adequate programming tasks
    D. do not need college education to do programming work

6. According to the above passage, data to be processed by computer should be   6._____

    A. recent   B. basic
    C. complete   D. verified

Questions 7-10.

DIRECTIONS: Questions 7 through 10 are to be answered SOLELY on the basis of the follow-
              ing passage.

There is nothing that will take the place of good sense on the part of the stenographer.
You may be perfect in transcribing exactly what the dictator says and your speed may be adequate, but without an understanding of the dictator's intent as well as his words, you are likely
to be a mediocre secretary.

A serious error that is made when taking dictation is putting down something that does
not make sense. Most people who dictate material would rather be asked to repeat and
explain than to receive transcribed material which has errors due to inattention or doubt.
Many dictators request that their grammar be corrected by their secretaries, but unless specifically asked to do so, secretaries should not do it without first checking with the dictator.
Secretaries should be aware that, in some cases, dictators may use incorrect grammar or
slang expressions to create a particular effect.

Some people dictate commas, periods, and paragraphs, while others expect the stenographer to know when, where, and how to punctuate. A well-trained secretary should be able
to indicate the proper punctuation by listening to the pauses and tones of the dictator's voice.

A stenographer who has taken dictation from the same person for a period of time should
be able to understand him under most conditions, By increasing her tact, alertness, and efficiency, a secretary can become more competent.

7. According to the above passage, which of the following statements concerning the dicta-   7._____
    tion of punctuation is CORRECT?

    A. Dictator may use incorrect punctuation to create a desired style
    B. Dictator should indicate all punctuation
    C. Stenographer should know how to punctuate based on the pauses and tones of
        the dictator
    D. Stenographer should not type any punctuation if it has not been dictated to her

8. According to the above passage, how should secretaries handle grammatical errors in a dictation? Secretaries should

    A. *not correct* grammatical errors unless the dictator is aware that this is being done
    B. *correct* grammatical errors by having the dictator repeat the line with proper pauses
    C. *correct* grammatical errors if they have checked the correctness in a grammar book
    D. *correct* grammatical errors based on their own good sense

8.____

9. If a stenographer is confused about the method of spacing and indenting of a report which has just been dictated to her, she GENERALLY should

    A. do the best she can
    B. ask the dictator to explain what she should do
    C. try to improve her ability to understand dictated material
    D. accept the fact that her stenographic ability is not adequate

9.____

10. In the last line of the first paragraph, the word *mediocre* means MOST NEARLY

    A. superior
    B. respected
    C. disregarded
    D. second-rate

10.____

Questions 11-12.

DIRECTIONS: Questions 11 and 12 are to be answered SOLELY on the basis of the following passage.

The number of legible carbon copies required to be produced determines the weight of the carbon paper to be used. When only one copy is made, heavy carbon paper is satisfactory. Most typists, however, use medium-weight carbon paper and find it serviceable for up to three or four copies. If five or more copies are to be made, it is wise to use light carbon paper. On the other hand, the finish of carbon paper to be used depends largely on the stroke of the typist and, in lesser degree, on the number of copies to be made and on whether the typewriter has pica or elite type. A soft-finish carbon paper should be used if the typist's touch is light or if a noiseless machine is used. It is desirable for the average typist to use medium-finish carbon paper for ordinary work, when only a few carbon copies are required. Elite type requires a harder carbon finish than pica type for the same number of copies.

11. According to the above passage, the lighter the carbon paper used,

    A. the softer the finish of the carbon paper will be
    B. the greater the number of legible carbon copies that can be made
    C. the greater the number of times the carbon paper can be used
    D. the lighter the typist's touch should be

11.____

12. According to the above passage, the MOST important factor which determines whether the finish of carbon paper to be used in typing should be hard, medium, or soft is

    A. the touch of the typist
    B. the number of carbon copies required
    C. whether the type in the typewriter is pica or elite
    D. whether a machine with pica type will produce the same number of carbon copies as a machine with elite type

12.____

Questions 13-16.

DIRECTIONS: Questions 13 through 16 are to be answered SOLELY on the basis of the following passage.

Modern office methods, geared to ever higher speeds and aimed at ever greater efficiency, are largely the result of the typewriter. The typewriter is a substitute for handwriting and, in the hands of a skilled typist, not only turns out letters and other documents at least three times faster than a penman can do the work, but turns out the greater volume more uniformly and legibly. With the use of carbon paper and onionskin paper, identical copies can be made at the same time.

The typewriter, besides its effect on the conduct of business and government, has had a very important effect on the position of women. The typewriter has done much to bring women into business and government, and today there are vastly more women than men typists. Many women have used the keys of the typewriter to climb the ladder to responsible managerial positions.

The typewriter, as its name implies, employs type to make an ink impression on paper. For many years, the manual typewriter was the standard machine used. Today, the electric typewriter is dominant, and completely automatic electronic typewriters are coming into wider use.

The mechanism of the office manual typewriter includes a set of keys arranged systematically in rows; a semicircular frame of type, connected to the keys by levers; the carriage, or paper carrier; a rubber roller, called a platen, against which the type strikes; and an inked ribbon which make the impression of the type character when the key strikes it.

13. The above passage mentions a number of good features of the combination of a skilled typist and a typewriter. Of the following, the feature which is NOT mentioned in the passage is   13._____

    A. speed
    C. uniformity
    B. reliability
    D. legibility

14. According to the above passage, a skilled typist can   14._____

    A. turn out at least five carbon copies of typed matter
    B. type at least three times faster than a penman can write
    C. type more than 80 words a minute
    D. readily move into a managerial position

15. According to the above passage, which of the following is NOT part of the mechanism of a manual typewriter?   15._____

    A. Carbon paper
    C. Paper carrier
    B. Platen
    D. Inked ribbon

16. According to the above passage, the typewriter has helped   16._____

    A. men more than women in business
    B. women in career advancement into management
    C. men and women equally, but women have taken better advantage of it
    D. more women than men, because men generally dislike routine typing work

Questions 17-21.

DIRECTIONS: Questions 17 through 21 are to be answered SOLELY on the basis of the following passage.

The recipient gains an impression of a typewritten letter before he begins to read the message. Factors which provide for a good first impression include margins and spacing that are visually pleasing, formal parts of the letter which are correctly placed according to the style of the letter, copy which is free of obvious erasures and over-strikes, and transcript that is even and clear. The problem for the typist is that of how to produce that first, positive impression of her work.

There are several general rules which a typist can follow when she wishes to prepare a properly spaced letter on a sheet of letterhead. Ordinarily, the width of a letter should not be less than four inches nor more than six inches. The side margins should also have a desirable relation to the bottom margin and the space between the letterhead and the body of the letter. Usually the most appealing arrangement is when the side margins are even and the bottom margin is slightly wider than the side margins. In some offices, however, standard line length is used for all business letters, and the secretary then varies the spacing between the date line and the inside address according to the length of the letter.

17. The BEST title for the above passage would be   17._____

    A. WRITING OFFICE LETTERS
    B. MAKING GOOD FIRST IMPRESSIONS
    C. JUDGING WELL-TYPED LETTERS
    D. GOOD PLACING AND SPACING FOR OFFICE LETTERS

18. According to the above passage, which of the following might be considered the way in   18._____
    which people very quickly judge the quality of work which has been typed? By

    A. measuring the margins to see if they are correct
    B. looking at the spacing and cleanliness of the typescript
    C. scanning the body of the letter for meaning
    D. reading the date line and address for errors

19. What, according to the above passage, would be definitely UNDESIRABLE as the aver-   19._____
    age line length of a typed letter?

    A. 4"   B. 6"
    C. 5"   D. 7"

20. According to the above passage, when the line length is kept standard, the secretary   20._____

    A. does not have to vary the spacing at all since this also is standard
    B. adjusts the spacing between the date line and inside address for different lengths
        of letters
    C. uses the longest line as a guideline for spacing between the date line and inside
        address
    D. varies-the number of spaces between the lines

21. According to the above passage, side margins are MOST pleasing when they   21.____

    A.   are even and somewhat smaller than the bottom margin
    B.   are slightly wider than the bottom margin
    C.   vary with the length of the letter
    D.   are figured independently from the letterhead and the body of the letter

Questions 22-25.

DIRECTIONS: Questions 22 through 25 are to be answered SOLELY on the basis of the following passage.

Typed pages can reflect the simplicity of modern art in a machine age. Lightness and evenness can be achieved by proper layout and balance of typed lines and white space. Instead of solid, cramped masses of uneven, crowded typing, there should be a pleasing balance up and down as well as horizontal.

To have real balance, your page must have a center. The eyes see the center of the sheet slightly above the real center. This is the way both you and the reader see it. Try imagining a line down the center of the page that divides the paper in equal halves. On either side of your paper, white space and blocks of typing need to be similar in size and shape. Although left and right margins should be equal, top and bottom margins need not be as exact. It looks better to hold a bottom border wider than a top margin, so that your typing rests upon a cushion of white space. To add interest to the appearance of the page, try making one paragraph between one-half and two-thirds the size of an adjacent paragraph.

Thus, by taking full advantage of your typewriter, the pages that you type will not only be accurate but will also be attractive.

22. It can be inferred from the above passage that the basic importance of proper balancing on a typed page is that proper balancing   22.____

    A.   makes a typed page a work of modern art
    B.   provides exercise in proper positioning of a typewriter
    C.   increases the amount of typed copy on the paper
    D.   draws greater attention and interest to the page

23. A reader will tend to see the center of a typed page   23.____

    A.   somewhat higher than the true center
    B.   somewhat lower than the true center
    C.   on either side of the true center
    D.   about two-thirds of an inch above the true center

24. Which of the following suggestions is NOT given by the above passage?   24.____

    A.   Bottom margins may be wider than top borders.
    B.   Keep all paragraphs approximately the same size.
    C.   Divide your page with an imaginary line down the middle.
    D.   Side margins should be equalized.

25. Of the following, the BEST title for the above passage is   25._____
    A. INCREASING THE ACCURACY OF THE TYPED PAGE
    B. DETERMINATION OF MARGINS FOR TYPED COPY
    C. LAYOUT AND BALANCE OF THE TYPED PAGE
    D. HOW TO TAKE FULL ADVANTAGE OF THE TYPEWRITER

KEY (CORRECT ANSWERS)

1.	C	11.	B
2.	A	12.	A
3.	B	13.	C
4.	A	14.	B
5.	D	15.	A
6.	D	16.	B
7.	C	17.	D
8.	A	18.	B
9.	B	19.	D
10.	D	20.	B

21.	A
22.	D
23.	A
24.	B
25.	C

TEST 3

DIRECTIONS: Each question or incomplete statement is followed by several suggested answers or completions. Select the one that BEST answers the question or completes the statement. *PRINT THE LETTER OF THE CORRECT ANSWER IN THE SPACE AT THE RIGHT.*

Questions 1-5.

DIRECTIONS: Questions 1 through 5 are to be answered SOLELY on the basis of the following passage.

A written report is a communication of information from one person to another. It is an account of some matter especially investigated, however routine that matter may be. The ultimate basis of any good written report is facts, which become known through observation and verification. Good written reports may seem to be no more than general ideas and opinions. However, in such cases, the facts leading to these opinions were gathered, verified, and reported earlier, and the opinions are dependent upon these facts. Good style, proper form, and emphasis cannot make a good written report out of unreliable information and bad judgment; but on the other hand, solid investigation and brilliant thinking are not likely to become very useful until they are effectively communicated to others. If a person's work calls for written reports, then his work is often no better than his written reports.

1. Based on the information in the above passage, it can be concluded that opinions expressed in a report should be

   A. based on facts which are gathered and reported
   B. emphasized repeatedly when they result from a special investigation
   C. kept to a minimum
   D. separated from the body of the report

2. In the above passage, the one of the following which is mentioned as a way of establishing facts is

   A. authority   B. reporting
   C. communication   D. verification

3. According to the above passage, the characteristic shared by ALL written reports is that they are

   A. accounts of routine matters   B. transmissions of information
   C. reliable and logical   D. written in proper form

4. Which of the following conclusions can logically be drawn from the information given in the above passage?

   A. Brilliant thinking can make up for unreliable information in a report.
   B. One method of judging an individual's work is the quality of the written reports he is required to submit.
   C. Proper form and emphasis can make a good report out of unreliable information.
   D. Good written reports that seem to be no more than general ideas should be rewritten.

5. Which of the following suggested titles would be MOST appropriate for the above pas-   5.___
sage?

   A. GATHERING AND ORGANIZING FACTS
   B. TECHNIQUES OF OBSERVATION
   C. NATURE AND PURPOSE OF REPORTS
   D. REPORTS AND OPINIONS: DIFFERENCES AND SIMILARITIES

Questions 6-8.

DIRECTIONS: Questions 6 through 8 are to be answered SOLELY on the basis of the following passage.

The most important unit of the mimeograph machine is a perforated metal drum over
which is stretched a cloth ink pad. A reservoir inside the drum contains the ink which flows
through the perforations and saturates the ink pad. To operate the machine, the operator first
removes from the machine the protective sheet, which keeps the ink from drying while the
machine is not in use. He then hooks the stencil face down on the drum, draws the stencil
smoothly over the drum, and fastens the stencil at the bottom. The speed with which the
drum turns determines the blackness of the copies printed. Slow turning gives heavy, black
copies; fast turning gives light, clear-cut reproductions. If reproductions are run on other than
porous paper, slip-sheeting is necessary to prevent smearing. Often, the printed copy fails to
drop readily as it comes from the machine. This may be due to static electricity. To remedy
this difficulty, the operator fastens a strip of tinsel from side to side near the impression roller
so that the printed copy just touches the soft stems of the tinsel as it is ejected from the
machine, thus grounding the static electricity to the frame of the machine.

6. According to the above passage,   6.___

   A. turning the drum fast produces light copies
   B. stencils should be placed face up on the drum
   C. ink pads should be changed daily
   D. slip-sheeting is necessary when porous paper is being used

7. According to the above passage, when a mimeograph machine is not in use,   7.___

   A. the ink should be drained from the drum
   B. the ink pad should be removed
   C. the machine should be covered with a protective sheet
   D. the counter should be set at zero

8. According to the above passage, static electricity is grounded to the frame of the mimeo-   8.___
graph machine by means of

   A. a slip-sheeting device
   B. a strip of tinsel
   C. an impression roller
   D. hooks located at the top of the drum

Questions 9-10.

DIRECTIONS: Questions 9 and 10 are to be answered SOLELY on the basis of the following passage.

The proofreading of material typed from copy is performed more accurately and more speedily when two persons perform this work as a team. The person who did not do the typing should read aloud the original copy while the person who did the typing should check the reading against the typed copy. The reader should speak very slowly and repeat the figures, using a different grouping of numbers when repeating the figures. For example, in reading 1967, the reader may say *one-nine-six-seven* on first reading the figure and *nineteen-sixty-seven* on repeating the figure. The reader should read all punctuation marks, taking nothing for granted. Since mistakes can occur anywhere, everything typed should be proofread. To avoid confusion, the proofreading team should use the standard proofreading marks, which are given in most dictionaries.

9. According to the above passage, the   9.____

   A. person who holds the typed copy is called the reader
   B. two members of a proofreading team should take turns in reading the typed copy aloud
   C. typed copy should be checked by the person who did the typing
   D. person who did not do the typing should read aloud from the typed copy

10. According to the above passage,   10.____

   A. it is unnecessary to read the period at the end of a sentence
   B. typographical errors should be noted on the original copy
   C. each person should develop his own set of proofreading marks
   D. figures should be read twice

Questions 11-16.

DIRECTIONS: Questions 11 through 16 are to be answered SOLELY on the basis of the above passage.

Basic to every office is the need for proper lighting. Inadequate lighting is a familiar cause of fatigue and serves to create a somewhat dismal atmosphere in the office. One requirement of proper lighting is that it be of an appropriate intensity. Intensity is measured in foot candles. According to the Illuminating Engineering Society of New York, for casual seeing tasks such as in reception rooms, inactive file rooms, and other service areas, it is recommended that the amount of light be 30 foot-candles. For ordinary seeing tasks such as reading, work in active file rooms, and in mailrooms, the recommended lighting is 100 foot-candles. For very difficult seeing tasks such as accounting, transcribing, and business machine use, the recommended lighting is 150 foot-candles.

Lighting intensity is only one requirement. Shadows and glare are to be avoided. For example, the larger the proportion of a ceiling filled with lighting units, the more glare-free and comfortable the lighting will be. Natural lighting from windows is not too dependable because on dark wintry days, windows yield little usable light, and on sunny summer afternoons, the glare from windows may be very distracting. Desks should not face the windows. Finally, the main lighting source ought to be overhead and to the left of the user,

11. According to the above passage, insufficient light in the office may cause   11._____

    A. glare   B. tiredness
    C. shadows   D. distraction

12. Based on the above passage, which of the following must be considered when planning   12._____
lighting arrangements? The

    A. amount of natural light present
    B. amount of work to be done
    C. level of difficulty of work to be done
    D. type of activity to be carried out

13. It can be inferred from the above passage that a well-coordinated lighting scheme is   13._____
LIKELY to result in

    A. greater employee productivity
    B. elimination of light reflection
    C. lower lighting cost
    D. more use of natural light

14. Of the following, the BEST title for the above passage is   14._____

    A. CHARACTERISTICS OF LIGHT
    B. LIGHT MEASUREMENT DEVICES
    C. FACTORS TO CONSIDER WHEN PLANNING LIGHTING SYSTEMS
    D. COMFORT VS. COST WHEN DEVISING LIGHTING ARRANGEMENTS

15. According to the above passage, a foot-candle is a measurement of the   15._____

    A. number of bulbs used
    B. strength of the light
    C. contrast between glare and shadow
    D. proportion of the ceiling filled with lighting units

16. According to the above passage, the number of foot-candles of light that would be   16._____
needed to copy figures onto a payroll is _____ foot-candles.

    A. less than 30   B. 100
    C. 30   D. 150

Questions 17-23.

DIRECTIONS: Questions 17 through 23 are to be answered SOLELY on the basis of the following passage, which is the Fee Schedule of a hypothetical college.

FEE SCHEDULE

A. A candidate for any baccalaureate degree is not required to pay tuition fees for undergraduate courses until he exceeds 128 credits, Candidates exceeding 128 credits in undergraduate courses are charged at the rate of $100 a credit for each credit of undergraduate course work in excess of 128. Candidates for a baccalaureate degree who are taking graduate courses must pay the same fee as any other student taking graduate courses

B. Non-degree students and college graduates are charged tuition fees for courses, whether undergraduate or graduate, at the rate of $180 a credit. For such students, there is an additional charge of $150 for each class hour per week in excess of the number of course credits. For example, if a three-credit course meets five hours a week, there is an additional charge for the extra two hours. Graduate courses are shown with a (G) before the course number.

C. All students are required to pay the laboratory fees indicated after the number of credits given for that course.

D. All students must pay a $250 general fee each semester.

E. Candidates for a baccalaureate degree are charged a $150 medical insurance fee for each semester. All other students are charged a $100 medical insurance fee each semester.

17. Miss Burton is not a candidate for a degree. She registers for the following courses in the spring semester: Economics 12, 4 hours a week, 3 credits; History (G) 23, 4 hours a week, 3 credits; English 1, 2 hours a week, 2 credits. The TOTAL amount in fees that Miss Burton must pay is   17.____

    A. less than $2000
    B. at least $2000 but less than $2100
    C. at least $2100 but less than $2200
    D. $2200 or over

18. Miss Gray is not a candidate for a degree. She registers for the following courses in the fall semester: History 3, 3 hours a week, 3 credits; English 5, 3 hours a week, 2 credits; Physics 5, 6 hours a week, 3 credits, laboratory fee $ 60; Mathematics 7, 4 hours a week, 3 credits. The TOTAL amount in fees that Miss Gray must pay is   18.____

    A. less than $3150
    B. at least $3150 but less than $3250
    C. at least $3250 but less than $3350
    D. $3350 or over

19. Mr. Wall is a candidate for the Bachelor of Arts degree and has completed 126 credits. He registers for the following courses in the spring semester, his final semester at college: French 4, 3 hours a week, 3 credits; Physics (G) 15, 6 hours a week, 3 credits, laboratory fee $80; History (G) 33, 4 hours a week, 3 credits. The TOTAL amount in fees that this candidate must pay is   19.____

    A. less than $2100
    B. at least $2100 but less than $2300
    C. at least $2300 but less than $2500
    D. $2500

20. Mr. Tindall, a candidate for the B.A. degree, has completed 122 credits of undergraduate courses. He registers for the following courses in his final semester: English 31, 3 hours a week, 3 credits; Philosophy 12, 4 hours a week, 4 credits; Anthropology 15, 3 hours a week, 3 credits; Economics (G) 68, 3 hours a week, 3 credits. The TOTAL amount in fees that Mr. Tindall must pay in his final semester is   20.____

    A. less than $1200
    B. at least $1200 but less than $1400
    C. at least $1400 but less than $1600
    D. $1600

21. Mr. Cantrell, who was graduated from the college a year ago, registers for graduate courses in the fall semester. Each course for which he registers carries the same number of credits as the number of hours a week it meets.
If he pays a total of $1530; including a $100 laboratory fee, the number of credits for which he is registered is

    A. 4   B. 5   C. 6   D. 7

21.____

22. Miss Jayson, who is not a candidate for a degree, has, registered for several courses including a lecture course in History. She withdraws from the course in History for which she had paid the required course fee of $690. The number of hours that this course is scheduled to meet is

    A. 4   B. 5   C. 2   D. 3

22.____

23. Mr. Van Arsdale, a graduate of a college is Iowa, registers for the following courses in one semester: Chemistry 35, 5 hours a week, 3 credits; Biology 13, 4 hours a week, 3 credits, laboratory fee $150; Mathematics (G) 179, 3 hours a week, 3 credits.
The TOTAL amount in fees that Mr. Van Arsdale must pay is

    A. less than $2400
    B. at least $2400 but less than $2500
    C. at least $2500 but less than $2600
    D. at least $2600 or over

23.____

Questions 24-25.

DIRECTIONS: Questions 24 and 25 are to be answered SOLELY on the basis of the following passage.

A duplex envelope is an envelope composed of two sections securely fastened together so that they become one mailing piece. This type of envelope makes it possible for a first class letter to be delivered simultaneously with third or fourth class matter and yet not require payment of the much higher first class postage rate on the entire mailing. First class postage is paid only on the letter which goes in the small compartment, third or fourth class postage being paid on the contents of the larger compartment. The larger compartment generally has an ungummed flap or clasp for sealing. The first class or smaller compartment has a gummed flap for sealing. Postal regulations require that the exact amount of postage applicable to each compartment be separately attached to it.

24. On the basis of the above passage, it is MOST accurate to state that

    A. the smaller compartment is placed inside the larger compartment before mailing
    B. the two compartments may be detached and mailed separately
    C. two classes of mailing matter may be mailed as a unit at two different postage rates
    D. the more expensive postage rate is paid on the matter in the larger compartment

24.____

25. When a duplex envelope is used, the 25.____

    A. first class compartment may be sealed with a clasp
    B. correct amount of postage must be placed on each compartment
    C. compartment containing third or fourth class mail requires a gummed flap for sealing
    D. full amount of postage for both compartments may be placed on the larger compartment

_____

KEY (CORRECT ANSWERS)

1.	A		11.	C
2.	D		12.	D
3.	B		13.	A
4.	B		14.	C
5.	C		15.	B
6.	A		16.	D
7.	C		17.	B
8.	B		18.	A
9.	C		19.	B
10.	D		20.	B

21. C
22. A
23. C
24. C
25. B

_____

EXAMINATION SECTION
TEST 1

DIRECTIONS: Each question or incomplete statement is followed by several suggested
answers of completions. Select the one that BEST answers the question or
completes the statement. *PRINT THE LETTER OF THE CORRECT ANSWER
IN THE SPACE AT THE RIGHT.*

1. One of the major objectives of a pre-employment interview is to get the interviewee to   1._____
respond freely to inquiries. The one of the following actions that would be *most likely* to
restrict the conversation of the interviewee would be for the investigator to
   A. keep a stenographic record of the interviewee's statements
   B. ask questions requiring complete explanations
   C. pose direct, specific questions to the interviewee
   D. allow the interviewee to respond to questions at his own pace

2. *One* of the reasons for the widespread use of the interview in personnel selection is that   2._____
the interview
   A. has been shown to be a valid measurement technique
   B. is efficient and reliable
   C. has been demonstrated to result in consistency among raters
   D. allows for flexibility of response

3. In conducting a personnel interview, which of the following guidelines would be MOST   3._____
desirable for the interviewer to follow?
   A. Allocate the same amount of time to each person being interviewed to standardize
   the process.
   B. Ask exactly the same questions of all persons being interviewed to increase the
   objectivity of the process.
   C. Eliminate the use of non-directive techniques because of their subjectivity.
   D. Vary his style and technique to fit the purpose of the interview and the people being
   interviewed.

4. You are planning to conduct preliminary interviews of applicants for an important position   4._____
in your department. Which of the following planning considerations is least *likely* to
contribute to successful interviews?
   A. Make provisions to conduct interviews in privacy.
   B. Schedule your appointments so that interviews will be short.
   C. Prepare a list of your objectives.
   D. Learn as much as you can about the applicant before the interview.

5. When dealing with an aggrieved worker, a USEFUL interviewing technique is to   5._____
   A. maintain a sympathetic attitude
   B. maintain an attitude of cold impartiality
   C. assure the subject that you are on his side
   D. display a tape recorder to give the subject confidence that no parts of his story
   will be overlooked

6. The "patterned interview" is a device used by sophisticated employers to   6._____
    A. select employees who fit the ethnic pattern of the community
    B. ascertain the pattern of facts surrounding a grievance
    C. discourage workers from joining unions
    D. appraise a subject's most important character traits

7. One of the applicants for a menial job is a tall, stooped, husky individual with a low   7._____
forehead, narrow eyes, a protruding chin, and a tendency to keep his mouth open.
In interviewing him, you *should*
    A. check him more carefully than the other applicants regarding criminal background
    B. disregard any skills he might have for other jobs which are vacant
    C. make your vocabulary somewhat simpler than with the other applicants
    D. make no assumptions regarding his ability on the basis of his appearance

8. Of the following, the BEST approach for you to use at the beginning of an interview with   8._____
a job applicant is to
    A. caution him to use his time economically and to get to the point
    B. ask him how long he intends to remain on the job if hired
    C. make some pleasant remarks to put him at ease
    D. emphasize the importance of the interview in obtaining the job

9. Of the following, the BEST reason for conducting an "exit interview" with an employee is to   9._____
    A. make certain that he returns all identification cards and office keys
    B. find out why he is leaving
    C. provide a useful training device for the exit interviewer
    D. discover if his initial hiring was in error

10. If you are to interview several applicants for jobs and rate them on five different factors   10._____
on a scale of 1 to 5, you should be MOST careful to *insure* that your
    A. rating on one factor does not influence your rating on another factor
    B. ratings on all factors are interrelated with a minimum of variation
    C. overall evaluation for employment exactly reflects the arithmetic average of your
       ratings
    D. overall evaluation for employment is unrelated to your individual ratings

11. Of the following, the question MOST appropriate for initial screening purposes generally is: 11._____
    A. What are your salary requirements?
    B. Why do you think you would like this kind of work?
    C. How did you get along with your last supervisor?
    D. What are your vocational goals?

12: Of the following, *normally* the question MOST appropriate for selection purposes generally   12._____
would tend to be:
    A. Where did you work last?
    B. When did you graduate from high. school?
    C. What was your average in school?
    D. Why did you select this organization?

13. Assume that you have been asked to interview each of several students who have been hired to work part-time. Which of the following would *ordinarily* be accomplished LEAST effectively in such-an interview?

    A. Providing information about the organization or institution in which the students will be Working.

    B. Directing the students to report for work each afternoon at specified times.

    C. Determining experience and background of the students so that appropriate assignments can be made.

    D. Changing the attitudes of the students toward the importance of parental controls.

13._____

14. In interviewing job applicants, which of the following usually does NOT have to be done before the end of the interview?

    A. Making a decision to hire an applicant.

    B. Securing information from applicants.

    C. Giving information to applicants.

    D. Establishing a friendly relationship with applicants.

14._____

15. In the process of interviewing applicants for a position on your staff, the *one* of the following which would be BEST is to

    A. make sure all applicants are introduced to the other members of your staff prior to the formal interview

    B. make sure the applicant does not ask questions about the job or the department

    C. avoid having the applicant talk with the staff under any circumstances

    D. introduce applicants to some of the staff at the conclusion of a successful interview

15._____

16. While interviewing a job applicant, you ask applicant left his last job. The applicant does not answer immediately.
Of the following, the BEST action to take at that point is to

    A. wait until he answers

    B. ask another question

    C. repeat the question in a loud voice

    D. ask him why he does not answer

16._____

17. You know that a student applying for a job in your office has done well in college except for two courses in science. However, when you ask him about his grades, his reply is vague and general.
It would be BEST for you to

    A. lead the applicant to admitting doing poorly in science to be sure that the facts are correct

    B. judge the applicant's tact and skill in handling what may be for him a personally sensitive question

    C. immediately confront the applicant with the facts and ask for an explanation

    D. ignore the applicant's response since you have the transcript

17._____

18. A college student has applied for a position with your department. Prior to conducting an interview of the job applicant, it would be LEAST helpful for you to have

    A. a personal resume

    B. a job description

    C. references

    D. hiring requirements

18._____

19. Job applicants tend to be nervous during interviews. Which of the following techniques   19._____
is *most likely* to put such an applicant at ease?
    A. Try to establish rapport by asking general questions which are easily answered by the applicant.
    B. Ask the applicant to describe his career objectives immediately, thus minimizing the anxiety caused by waiting.
    C. Start the interview with another member of the' staff present so that the applicant does not feel alone.
    D. Proceed as rapidly as possible, since the emotional state of the applicant is none of your concern.

20. At the first interview between a supervisor and a newly appointed subordinate,   20._____
GREATEST care should be taken to
    A. build toward a satisfactory personal relationship even if some other objectives of the interview must be postponed
    B. cover a predetermined list of specific objectives so as to make a further orientation interview unnecessary
    C. create an image of a forceful, determined supervisor whose wishes cannot be opposed by a subordinate without great risk
    D. create an impression of efficiency and control of operation free from interpersonal relationships

21. You are a supervisor in an agency and are holding your first interview with a new   21._____
employee. In this interview, you should strive MAINLY to
    A. show the new employee that you are an efficient and objective supervisor, with a completely impersonal attitude toward your subordinates
    B. complete the entire orientation process including the giving of detailed job-duty instructions
    C. make it clear to the employee that all your decisions are based on your many years of experience
    D. lay the groundwork for a good employee-supervisor relationship by gaining the new employee's confidence

22. The INCORRECT statement related to the principles of interviewing is: 22._____
    A. Written outlines should be avoided by the interviewer because they tend to be overly restrictive.
    B. Preliminary planning (for the interview) should involve an analysis of the point of view of the person to be interviewed.
    C. An interviewing supervisor should make every effort to conduct it in privacy to avoid possible inhibitions.
    D. Well-planned questions are sometimes necessary in conducting an interview.

23. Assume that you are conducting an interview with a prospective employee who is of   23._____
limited mental ability and low socio-economic status. Of the following, it is *most likely*
that asking him many open-ended questions about his work experience would cause
him to respond
    A. articulately   B. reluctantly
    C. comfortably   D. aggressively

24. An individual interview is to be used as part of an examination for a supervisory position. 24._____
Of the following, the attribute or characteristic that is LEAST suitable for evaluation in such an, interview is
   A. ability to supervise people
   B. poise and confidence
   C. response to stress conditions
   D. rigidity and flexibility

25. In conducting a disciplinary interview, a supervisor finds that he must ask some highly 25._____
personal questions which are relevant to the problem at hand. The interviewer is *most likely* to get TRUTHFUL answers to these questions if he asks them
   A. early in the interview, before the interviewee has had a chance to become emotional
   B. in a manner so that the interviewee can answer them with a simple "yes" or "no"
   C. well into the interview, after rapport and trust have been established
   D. just after the close of the interview, so that the questions appear to be off the record

KEY (CORRECT ANSWERS)

1. A		11. A	
2. D		12. D	
3. D		13. D	
4. B		14. A	
5. A		15. D	
6. D		16. A	
7. D		17. B	
8. C		18. C	
9. B		19. A	
10. A		20. A	

21. D
22. A
23. B
24. A
25. C

TEST 2

DIRECTIONS: Each question or incomplete statement is followed by several suggested answers of completions. Select the one that BEST answers the question or completes the statement. *PRINT THE LETTER OF THE CORRECT ANSWER IN THE SPACE AT THE RIGHT.*

1. Of the following methods of conducting an interview, the BEST is to   1._____
   A. ask questions with "yes" or "no" answers
   B. listen carefully and ask only questions that are pertinent
   C. fire questions at the interviewee so that he must answer sincerely and briefly
   D. read standardized questions to the person being interviewed

2. An interviewer should begin with topics which are easy to talk about and which are not   2._____
   threatening.
   This procedure is useful MAINLY because it
   A. allows the applicant a little time to get accustomed to the situation and leads to freer communication
   B. distracts the attention of the person being interviewed from the main purpose of the questioning
   C. is the best way for the interviewer to show that he is relaxed and confident on the job
   D. causes the interviewee to feel that the interviewer is apportioning valuable questioning time

3. The initial interview will normally be more of a problem to the interviewer than any   3._____
   subsequent interviews he may have with the same person because
   A. the interviewee is likely to be hostile
   B. there is too much to be accomplished in one session
   C. he has less information about the client than he will have later
   D. some information may be forgotten when later making record of this first interview

4. Most successful interviews are those in which the interviewer shows a genuine interest   4._____
   in the person he is questioning.
   This attitude would *most likely* cause the individual being interviewed to
   A. feel that the interviewer already knows all the facts in his case
   B. act more naturally and reveal more of his true feelings
   C. request that the interviewer give more attention to his problems, not his personality
   D. react defensively, suppress his negative feelings and conceal the real facts in his case

5. When interviewing a person, the interviewer may easily slip into error in rating his   5._____
   subject's personal qualities because of the general impression he receives of the individual.
   This tendency is known as the
   A. "halo" effect
   B. subjective bias problem
   C. "person-to-person" error
   D. inflation effect

6. An interviewer would find an interview check list LEAST useful for   6._____
   A. making sure that all the principal facts are secured in the interview
   B. insuring that the claimant's grievance is settled in his favor
   C. facilitating later research into the nature of the problems handled by the agency
   D. conducting the interview in a logical and orderly fashion

7. There are almost as many techniques of interviewing as there are interviewers.   7._____
   Of the following, the LEAST objectionable method is to
   A. ask if interviewee minds being quoted
   B. make occasional notes as important topics come up
   C. take notes unobtrusively
   D. take shorthand notes of every word

8. Questions worded so that the person being interviewed has some hint of the desired   8._____
   answer can modify the person's response. The result of the inclusion of such questions
   in an interview, even when they are used inadvertently, is to
   A. have no effect on the basic content of the information given by the person interviewed
   B. have value in convincing the person that the suggested plan is the best for him
   C. cause the person to give more meaningful information
   D. reduce the validity of the meaningful information obtained from the person

9. The person MOST likely to be a good interviewer is one who   9._____
   A. is able to outguess the person being interviewed
   B. tries to change the attitudes of the persons he interviews
   C. controls the interview by skillfully dominating the conversation
   D. is able to imagine himself in the position of the person being interviewed

10. The "halo effect" is an overall impression on the interviewee, whether favorable or   10._____
    unfavorable, usually created by a single trait. This impression then influences the
    appraisal of all other factors. A "halo effect" is *least likely* to be created at an
    interview where the interviewee is a
    A. person of average appearance and ability
    B. rough-looking man who uses abusive language
    C. young attractive woman being interviewed by a man
    D. person who demonstrates an exceptional ability to remember faces

11. Of the following, the BEST way for an interviewer to calm a person who seems to   11._____
    have become emotionally upset as a result of a question asked is for the interviewer to
    A. talk to the person about other things for a short time
    B. ask that the person control himself
    C. probe for the cause of his emotional upset
    D. finish the questioning as quickly as possible

12. Of the following, the GREATEST pitfall in interviewing is that the result may be   12._____
    affected by the
    A. bias of the interviewee
    B. bias of the interviewer
    C. educational level of the interviewee
    D. educational level of the interviewer

13. Assume you are assigned to interview applicants.   13.____
Of the following, which is the BEST attitude for you to take in dealing with applicants?
    A. Assume they will enjoy being interviewed because they believe that you have the power of decision
    B. Expect that they have a history of anti-social behavior in the family, and probe deeply into the social development of family members
    C. Expect that they will try to control the interview, thus you should keep them on the defensive
    D. Assume that they will be polite and cooperative and attempt to secure the information you need in a business-like manner

14. A Spanish-speaking applicant may want to bring his bilingual child with him to an   14.____
interview to act as an interpreter. 'Which of the following would be LEAST likely to
affect the value of an interview in which an applicant's child has acted as interpreter?
    A. It may make it undesirable to ask certain questions.
    B. A child may do an inadequate job of interpretation.
    C. A child's answers may indicate his feelings toward his parents.
    D. The applicant may not want to reveal all information in front of his child.

15. In answering questions asked by students, faculty, and the public, it is MOST   15.____
important that
    A. you indicate your source of information
    B. you are not held responsible for the answers
    C. the facts you give be accurate
    D. the answers cover every possible aspect of each question

16. Assume that someone you are interviewing is reluctant to give you certain information.   16.____
He would *probably* be MORE responsive if you show him that
    A. all the other persons you interviewed provided you with the information
    B. it would serve his own best interests to give you the information
    C. the information is very important to you
    D. you are business like and take a no-nonsense approach

17. Taking notes while you are interviewing someone is *most likely* to   17.____
    A. arouse doubts as to your trustworthiness
    B. give the interviewee confidence in your ability
    C. insure that you record the facts you think are important
    D. make the responses of the interviewee unreliable

18. In developing a role playing situation to be used to train interviewers, the one of the   18.____
following that it would be MOST IMPORTANT to use as a guide is that the situation
    A. allow the role player to identify readily with the role he is to play
    B. be free of actual or potential conflict between the role players
    C. can be clearly recognized by the participants as an actual interview situation that has already taken place
    D. should provide a detailed set of specifications for handling the roles to be played

19. Restating a question before the person being interviewed gives an answer to the
original question is usually NOT good practice *principally* because
    A. the client will think that you don't know your job
    B. it may confuse the client
    C. the interviewer should know exactly what to ask and how to put the question
    D. it reveals the interviewer's insecurity

19._____

20. In interviewing a man who has a grievance, it is IMPORTANT that the interviewer
    A. take note of such physical responses as shifty eyes
    B. use a lie detector, if possible, to ascertain the truth in doubtful situations
    C. allow the complainant to "tell his story"
    D. place the complainant under oath

20._____

21. Ideally, the setting for an interview should NOT include
    A. an informal opening
    B. privacy and comfort
    C. an atmosphere of leisure
    D. a lie detector

21.____

22. Which of the following is an example of a "non-directive" interview?
    A. The subject directs his remarks at someone other than the interviewer.
    B. The subject discusses any topics that seem to be relevant to him.
    C. The subject has not been directed that he need answer any particular questions.
    D. The interview is confined to the facts of the case and is not directed at eliciting
    personal information.

22._____

23. Of the following abilities, the one which is LEAST important in conducting an interview
is the ability to
    A. ask the interviewee pertinent questions
    B. evaluate the interviewee on the basis of appearance
    C. evaluate the responses of the interviewee
    D. gain the cooperation of the interviewee

23._____

24. Which of the following actions would be LEAST desirable for you to take when you
have to conduct an interview?
    A. Set a relaxed and friendly atmosphere.
    B. Plan you interview ahead of time.
    C. Allow the person interviewed to structure the interview as he wishes.
    D. Include some stock or standard question which you ask everyone.

24._____

25. One of the MOST important techniques for conducting good interviews is
    A. asking the applicant questions in rapid succession, thereby keeping the
    conversation properly focused
    B. listening carefully to all that the applicant has to say, making mental notes
    of possible areas for follow-up
    C. indicating to the applicant the criteria and standards on which you will base
    your judgment
    D. making sure that you are interrupted about five minutes before you wish to
    end so that you can keep on schedule

25._____

KEY (CORRECT ANSWERS)

1.	B		11.	A
2.	A		12.	B
3.	C		13.	D
4.	B		14.	C
5.	A		15.	C
6.	B		16.	B
7.	C		17.	C
8.	D		18.	A
9.	D		19.	B
10.	A		20.	C

21. D
22. B
23. B
24. C
25. B

———

PREPARING WRITTEN MATERIAL

EXAMINATION SECTION
TEST 1

DIRECTIONS: Each of the sentences in the Tests that follow may be classified under one of the following four categories:

     A.   *Faulty* because of incorrect grammar or word usage
     B.   *Faulty* because of incorrect punctuation
     C.   *Faulty* because of incorrect capitalization or incorrect spelling
     D.   *Correct*

     Examine each sentence carefully to determine under which of the above four options it is best classified. Then, in the space to the right, print the capital letter preceding the option which is the best of the four suggested above.

     (Note that each faulty sentence contains but one type of error. Consider a sentence to be correct if it contains none of the types of errors mentioned, even though there may be other correct ways of expressing the same thought.)

1.   He sent the notice to the clerk who you hired yesterday.   1._____

2.   It must be admitted, however that you were not informed of this change.   2._____

3.   Only the employees who have served in this grade for at least two years are eligible for promotion.   3._____

4.   The work was divided equally between she and Mary.   4._____

5.   He thought that you were not available at that time.   5._____

6.   When the messenger returns; please give him this package.   6._____

7.   The new secretary prepared, typed, addressed, and delivered, the notices.   7._____

8.   Walking into the room, his desk can be seen at the rear.   8._____

9.   Although John has worked here longer than She, he produces a smaller amount of work.   9._____

10.   She said she could of typed this report yesterday.   10._____

11.   Neither one of these procedures are adequate for the efficient performance of this task.   11._____

12.   The typewriter is the tool of the typist; the cash register, the tool of the cashier.   12._____

13.   "The assignment must be completed as soon as possible" said the supervisor.   13._____

14.   As you know, office handbooks are issued to all new Employees.   14._____

15.   Writing a speech is sometimes easier than to deliver it before an audience.   15._____

16.   Mr. Brown our accountant, will audit the accounts next week.   16._____

17. Give the assignment to whomever is able to do it most efficiently.   17.____

18. The supervisor expected either your or I to file these reports.   18.____

KEY (CORRECT ANSWERS)

1.	A		10.	A
2.	B		11.	A
3.	D		12.	C
4.	A		13.	B
5.	D		14.	C
6.	B		15.	A
7.	B		16.	B
8.	A		17.	A
9.	C		18.	A

TEST 2

DIRECTIONS: Each of the sentences in the Tests that follow may be classified under one of the following four categories:
- A. *Faulty* because of incorrect grammar or word usage
- B. *Faulty* because of incorrect punctuation
- C. *Faulty* because of incorrect capitalization or incorrect spelling
- D. *Correct*

Examine each sentence carefully to determine under which of the above four options it is best classified. Then, in the space to the right, print the capital letter preceding the option which is the best of the four suggested above.

(Note that each faulty sentence contains but one type of error. Consider a sentence to be correct if it contains none of the types of errors mentioned, even though there may be other correct ways of expressing the same thought.)

1. The fire apparently started in the storeroom, which is usually locked.   1._____

2. On approaching the victim, two bruises were noticed by this officer.   2._____

3. The officer, who was there examined the report with great care.   3._____

4. Each employee in the office had a seperate desk.   4._____

5. All employees including members of the clerical staff, were invited to the lecture.   5._____

6. The suggested Procedure is similar to the one now in use.   6._____

7. No one was more pleased with the new procedure than the chauffeur.   7._____

8. He tried to persaude her to change the procedure.   8._____

9. The total of the expenses charged to petty cash were high.   9._____

10. An understanding between him and I was finally reached.   10._____

_____

KEY (CORRECT ANSWERS)

1.	D	6.	C
2.	A	7.	D
3.	B	8.	C
4.	C	9.	A
5.	B	10.	A

———

TEST 3

DIRECTIONS: Each of the sentences in the Tests that follow may be classified under one of the following four categories:
    A. *Faulty* because of incorrect grammar or word usage
    B. *Faulty* because of incorrect punctuation
    C. *Faulty* because of incorrect capitalization or incorrect spelling
    D. *Correct*

Examine each sentence carefully to determine under which of the above four options it is best classified. Then, in the space to the right, print the capital letter preceding the option which is the best of the four suggested above.

(Note that each faulty sentence contains but one type of error. Consider a sentence to be correct if it contains none of the types of errors mentioned, even though there may be other correct ways of expressing the same thought.)

1. They told both he and I that the prisoner had escaped.   1._____

2. Any superior officer, who, disregards the just complaints of his subordinates, is remiss in the performance of his duty.   2._____

3. Only those members of the national organization who resided in the Middle West attended the conference in Chicago.   3._____

4. We told him to give the investigation assignment to whoever was available.   4._____

5. Please do not disappoint and embarass us by not appearing in court.   5._____

6. Although the officer's speech proved to be entertaining, the topic was not relevent to the main theme of the conference.   6._____

7. In February all new officers attended a training course in which they were learned in their principal duties and the fundamental operating procedures of the department.   7._____

8. I personally seen inmate Jones threaten inmates Smith and Green with bodily harm if they refused to participate in the plot.   8._____

9. To the layman, who on a chance visit to the prison observes everything functioning smoothly, the maintenance of prison discipline may seem to be a relatively easily realizable objective.   9._____

10. The prisoners in cell block fourty were forbidden to sit on the cell cots during the recreation hour.   10._____

KEY (CORRECT ANSWERS)

1.	A	6.	C
2.	B	7.	A
3.	C	8.	A
4.	D	9.	D
5.	C	10.	C

———

TEST 4

DIRECTIONS: Each of the sentences in the Tests that follow may be classified under one of the following four categories:
- A. *Faulty* because of incorrect grammar or word usage
- B. *Faulty* because of incorrect punctuation
- C. *Faulty* because of incorrect capitalization or incorrect spelling
- D. *Correct*

Examine each sentence carefully to determine under which of the above four options it is best classified. Then, in the space to the right, print the capital letter preceding the option which is the best of the four suggested above.

(Note that each faulty sentence contains but one type of error. Consider a sentence to be correct if it contains none of the types of errors mentioned, even though there may be other correct ways of expressing the same thought.)

1. I cannot encourage you any.   1.____

2. You always look well in those sort of clothes.   2.____

3. Shall we go to the park?   3.____

4. The man whome he introduced was Mr. Carey.   4.____

5. She saw the letter laying here this morning.   5.____

6. It should rain before the Afternoon is over.   6.____

7. They have already went home.   7.____

8. That Jackson will be elected is evident.   8.____

9. He does not hardly approve of us.   9.____

10. It was he, who won the prize.   10.____

———

KEY (CORRECT ANSWERS)

1.	A	6.	C
2.	A	7.	A
3.	D	8.	D
4.	C	9.	A
5.	A	10.	B

———

TEST 5

DIRECTIONS: Each of the sentences in the Tests that follow may be classified under one of the following four categories:
   A.   *Faulty* because of incorrect grammar or word usage
   B.   *Faulty* because of incorrect punctuation
   C.   *Faulty* because of incorrect capitalization or incorrect spelling
   D.   *Correct*

   Examine each sentence carefully to determine under which of the above four options it is best classified. Then, in the space to the right, print the capital letter preceding the option which is the best of the four suggested above.

   (Note that each faulty sentence contains but one type of error. Consider a sentence to be correct if it contains none of the types of errors mentioned, even though there may be other correct ways of expressing the same thought.)

1.   Shall we go to the park.   1._____

2.   They are, alike, in this particular way.   2._____

3.   They gave the poor man sume food when he knocked on the door.   3._____

4.   I regret the loss caused by the error.   4._____

5.   The students' will have a new teacher.   5._____

6.   They sweared to bring out all the facts.   6._____

7.   He decided to open a branch store on 33rd street.   7._____

8.   His speed is equal and more than that of a racehorse.   8._____

9.   He felt very warm on that Summer day.   9._____

10.   He was assisted by his friend, who lives in the next house.   10._____

KEY (CORRECT ANSWERS)

1.	B	6.	A
2.	B	7.	C
3.	C	8.	A
4.	D	9.	C
5.	B	10.	D

———

TEST 6

DIRECTIONS: Each of the sentences in the Tests that follow may be classified under one of the following four categories:
- A. *Faulty* because of incorrect grammar or word usage
- B. *Faulty* because of incorrect punctuation
- C. *Faulty* because of incorrect capitalization or incorrect spelling
- D. *Correct*

Examine each sentence carefully to determine under which of the above four options it is best classified. Then, in the space to the right, print the capital letter preceding the option which is the best of the four suggested above.

(Note that each faulty sentence contains but one type of error. Consider a sentence to be correct if it contains none of the types of errors mentioned, even though there may be other correct ways of expressing the same thought.)

1. The climate of New York is colder than California.   1._____

2. I shall wait for you on the corner.   2._____

3. Did we see the boy who, we think, is the leader.   3._____

4. Being a modest person, John seldom talks about his invention.   4._____

5. The gang is called the smith street boys.   5._____

6. He seen the man break into the store.   6._____

7. We expected to lay still there for quite a while.   7._____

8. He is considered to be the Leader of his organization.   8._____

9. Although I recieved an invitation, I won't go.   9._____

10. The letter must be here some place.   10._____

KEY (CORRECT ANSWERS)

1.	A		6.	A
2.	D		7.	A
3.	B		8.	C
4.	D		9.	C
5.	C		10.	A

———

TEST 7

DIRECTIONS: Each of the sentences in the Tests that follow may be classified under one of the following four categories:
   A. *Faulty* because of incorrect grammar or word usage
   B. *Faulty* because of incorrect punctuation
   C. *Faulty* because of incorrect capitalization or incorrect spelling
   D. *Correct*

   Examine each sentence carefully to determine under which of the above four options it is best classified. Then, in the space to the right, print the capital letter preceding the option which is the best of the four suggested above.

   (Note that each faulty sentence contains but one type of error. Consider a sentence to be correct if it contains none of the types of errors mentioned, even though there may be other correct ways of expressing the same thought.)

1. I though it to be he.   1._____

2. We expect to remain here for a long time.   2._____

3. The committee was agreed.   3._____

4. Two-thirds of the building are finished.   4._____

5. The water was froze.   5._____

6. Everyone of the salesmen must supply their own car.   6._____

7. Who is the author of Gone With the Wind?   7._____

8. He marched on and declaring that he would never surrender.   8._____

9. Who shall I say called?   9._____

10. Everyone has left but they.   10._____

KEY (CORRECT ANSWERS)

1.	A	6.	A
2.	D	7.	B
3.	D	8.	A
4.	A	9.	D
5.	A	10.	D

———

TEST 8

DIRECTIONS: Each of the sentences in the Tests that follow may be classified under one of the following four categories:
   A.   *Faulty* because of incorrect grammar or word usage
   B.   *Faulty* because of incorrect punctuation
   C.   *Faulty* because of incorrect capitalization or incorrect spelling
   D.   *Correct*

   Examine each sentence carefully to determine under which of the above four options it is best classified. Then, in the space to the right, print the capital letter preceding the option which is the best of the four suggested above.

   (Note that each faulty sentence contains but one type of error. Consider a sentence to be correct if it contains none of the types of errors mentioned, even though there may be other correct ways of expressing the same thought.)

1.   Who did we give the order to?   1.____

2.   Send your order in immediately.   2.____

3.   I believe I paid the Bill.   3.____

4.   I have not met but one person.   4.____

5.   Why aren't Tom, and Fred, going to the dance?   5.____

6.   What reason is there for him not going?   6.____

7.   The seige of Malta was a tremendous event.   7.____

8.   I was there yesterday I assure you.   8.____

9.   Your ukelele is better than mine.   9.____

10. No one was there only Mary.   10.____

KEY (CORRECT ANSWERS)

1.	A	6.	A
2.	D	7.	C
3.	C	8.	B
4.	A	9.	C
5.	B	10.	A

———

TEST 9

DIRECTIONS: In each of the following groups of sentences, one of the four sentences is faulty in grammar, punctuation, or capitalization. Select the incorrect sentence in each case.

1. A. If you had stood at home and done your homework, you would not have failed in arithmetic.   1.____
    B. Her affected manner annoyed every member of the audience.
    C. How will the new law affect our income taxes?
    D. The plants were not affected by the long, cold winter, but they succumbed to the drought of summer.

2. A. He is one of the most able men who have been in the Senate.   2.____
    B. It is he who is to blame for the lamentable mistake.
    C. Haven't you a helpful suggestion to make at this time?
    D. The money was robbed from the blind man's cup.

3. A. The amount of children in this school is steadily increasing.   3.____
    B. After taking an apple from the table, she went out to play.
    C. He borrowed a dollar from me.
    D. I had hoped my brother would arrive before me.

4. A. Whom do you think I hear from every week?   4.____
    B. Who do you think is the right man for the job?
    C. Who do you think I found in the room?
    D. He is the man whom we considered a good candidate for the presidency.

5. A. Quietly the puppy laid down before the fireplace.   5.____
    B. You have made your bed; now lie in it.
    C. I was badly sunburned because I had lain too long in the sun.
    D. I laid the doll on the bed and left the room.

_____

KEY (CORRECT ANSWERS)

1. A
2. D
3. A
4. C
5. A

PREPARING WRITTEN MATERIAL

PARAGRAPH REARRANGEMENT
COMMENTARY

The sentences which follow are in scrambled order. You are to rearrange them in proper order and indicate the letter choice containing the correct answer at the space at the right.

Each group of sentences in this section is actually a paragraph presented in scrambled order. Each sentence in the group has a place in that paragraph; no sentence is to be left out. You are to read each group of sentences and decide upon the best order in which to put the sentences so as to form as well-organized paragraph.

The questions in this section measure the ability to solve a problem when all the facts relevant to its solution are not given.

More specifically, certain positions of responsibility and authority require the employee to discover connections between events sometimes, apparently, unrelated. In order to do this, the employee will find it necessary to correctly infer that unspecified events have probably occurred or are likely to occur. This ability becomes especially important when action must be taken on incomplete information.

Accordingly, these questions require competitors to choose among several suggested alternatives, each of which presents a different sequential arrangement of the events. Competitors must choose the MOST logical of the suggested sequences.

In order to do so, they may be required to draw on general knowledge to infer missing concepts or events that are essential to sequencing the given events. Competitors should be careful to infer only what is essential to the sequence. The plausibility of the wrong alternatives will always require the inclusion of unlikely events or of additional chains of events which are NOT essential to sequencing the given events.

It's very important to remember that you are looking for the best of the four possible choices, and that the best choice of all may not even be one of the answers you're given to choose from.

There is no one right way to solve these problems. Many people have found it helpful to first write out the order of the sentences, as they would have arranged them, on their scrap paper before looking at the possible answers. If their optimum answer is there, this can save them some time. If it isn't, this method can still give insight into solving the problem. Others find it most helpful to just go through each of the possible choices, contrasting each as they go along. You should use whatever method feels comfortable, and works, for you.

While most of these types of questions are not that difficult, we've added a higher percentage of the difficult type, just to give you more practice. Usually there are only one or two questions on this section that contain such subtle distinctions that you're unable to answer confidently, and you then may find yourself stuck deciding between two possible choices, neither of which you're sure about.

EXAMINATION SECTION
TEST 1

DIRECTIONS: The sentences that follow are in scrambled order. You are to rearrange them in proper order and indicate the letter choice containing the correct answer. *PRINT THE LETTER OF THE CORRECT ANSWER IN THE SPACE AT THE RIGHT.*

1.   Below are four statements labeled W., X., Y., and Z.   1.____
     W.   He was a strict and fanatic drillmaster.
     X.   The word is always used in a derogatory sense and generally shows resent-
           ment and anger on the part of the user.
     Y.   It is from the name of this Frenchman that we derive our English word, martinet.
     Z.   Jean Martinet was the Inspector-General of Infantry during the reign of King
           Louis XIV.
     The *PROPER* order in which these sentences should be placed in a paragraph is:

     A. X, Z, W, Y   B. X, Z, Y, W   C. Z, W, Y, X   D. Z, Y, W, X

2.   In the following paragraph, the sentences which are numbered, have been jumbled.   2.____
     1.   Since then it has undergone changes.
     2.   It was incorporated in 1955 under the laws of the State of New York.
     3.   Its primary purpose, a cleaner city, has, however, remained the same.
     4.   The Citizens Committee works in cooperation with the Mayor's Inter-departmen-
           tal Committee for a Clean City.
     The order in which these sentences should be arranged to form a well-organized para-
     graph is:

     A. 2, 4, 1, 3   B. 3, 4, 1, 2   C. 4, 2, 1, 3   D. 4, 3, 2, 1

Questions 3-5.

DIRECTIONS: The sentences listed below are part of a meaningful paragraph but they are not given in their proper order. You are to decide what would be the *best order* in which to put the sentences so as to form a well-organized paragraph. Each sentence has a place in the paragraph; there are no extra sentences. You are then to answer questions 3 to 5 inclusive on the basis of your rearrangements of these scrambled sentences into a properly organized paragraph.

In 1887 some insurance companies organized an Inspection Department to advise their clients on all phases of fire prevention and protection. Probably this has been due to the smaller annual fire losses in Great Britain than in the United States. It tests various fire prevention devices and appliances and determines manufacturing hazards and their safeguards. Fire research began earlier in the United States and is more advanced than in Great Britain. Later they established a laboratory specializing in electrical, mechanical, hydraulic, and chemical fields.

3. When the five sentences are arranged in proper order, the paragraph starts with the sentence which begins

    A. "In 1887..."   B. "Probably this ..."   C. "It tests ..."
    D. "Fire research ..." E. "Later they ..."

3.____

4. In the last sentence listed above, "they" refers to

    A. insurance companies
    B. the United States and Great Britain
    C. the Inspection Department
    D. clients
    E. technicians

4.____

5. When the above paragraph is properly arranged, it ends with the words

    A. "... and protection."   B. "... the United States."
    C. "... their safeguards."   D. "... in Great Britain."
    E. "... chemical fields."

5.____

KEY (CORRECT ANSWERS)

1. C
2. C
3. D
4. A
5. C

TEST 2

DIRECTIONS: In each of the questions numbered 1 through 5, several sentences are given. For each question, choose as your answer the group of numbers that represents the *most logical* order of these sentences if they were arranged in paragraph form. *PRINT THE LETTER OF THE CORRECT ANSWER IN THE SPACE AT THE RIGHT.*

1.
1. It is established when one shows that the landlord has prevented the tenant's enjoyment of his interest in the property leased.
2. Constructive eviction is the result of a breach of the covenant of quiet enjoyment implied in all leases.
3. In some parts of the United States, it is not complete until the tenant vacates within a reasonable time.
4. Generally, the acts must be of such serious and permanent character as to deny the tenant the enjoyment of his possessing rights.
5. In this event, upon abandonment of the premises, the tenant's liability for that ceases.

The CORRECT answer is:

A. 2, 1, 4, 3, 5   B. 5, 2, 3, 1, 4   C. 4, 3, 1, 2, 5
D. 1, 3, 5, 4, 2

1.____

2.
1. The powerlessness before private and public authorities that is the typical experience of the slum tenant is reminiscent of the situation of blue-collar workers all through the nineteenth century.
2. Similarly, in recent years, this chapter of history has been reopened by anti-poverty groups which have attempted to organize slum tenants to enable them to bargain collectively with their landlords about the conditions of their tenancies.
3. It is familiar history that many of the workers remedied their condition by joining together and presenting their demands collectively.
4. Like the workers, tenants are forced by the conditions of modern life into substantial dependence on these who possess great political arid economic power.
5. What's more, the very fact of dependence coupled with an absence of education and self-confidence makes them hesitant and unable to stand up for what they need from those in power.

The CORRECT answer is:

A. 5, 4, 1, 2, 3   B. 2, 3, 1, 5, 4   C. 3, 1, 5, 4, 2
D. 1, 4, 5, 3, 2

2.____

3.
1. A railroad, for example, when not acting as a common carrier may contract away responsibility for its own negligence.
2. As to a landlord, however, no decision has been found relating to the legal effect of a clause shifting the statutory duty of repair to the tenant.
3. The courts have not passed on the validity of clauses relieving the landlord of this duty and liability.
4. They have, however, upheld the validity of exculpatory clauses in other types of contracts.
5. Housing regulations impose a duty upon the landlord to maintain leased premises in safe condition.

3.____

6. As another example, a bailee may limit his liability except for gross negligence, willful acts, or fraud.

The CORRECT answer is:

A. 2, 1, 6, 4, 3, 5   B. 1, 3, 4, 5, 6, 2   C. 3, 5, 1, 4, 2, 6
D. 5, 3, 4, 1, 6, 2

4.
1. Since there are only samples in the building, retail or consumer sales are generally eschewed by mart occupants, and in some instances, rigid controls are maintained to limit entrance to the mart only to those persons engaged in retailing.
2. Since World War I, in many larger cities, there has developed a new type of property, called the mart building.
3. It can, therefore, be used by wholesalers and jobbers for the display of sample merchandise.
4. This type of building is most frequently a multi-storied, finished interior property which is a cross between a retail arcade and a loft building.
5. This limitation enables the mart occupants to ship the orders from another location after the retailer or dealer makes his selection from the samples.

4.____

The CORRECT answer is:

A. 2, 4, 3, 1, 5   B. 4, 3, 5, 1, 2   C. 1, 3, 2, 4, 5
D. 1, 4, 2, 3, 5

5.
1. In general, staff-line friction reduces the distinctive contribution of staff personnel.
2. The conflicts, however, introduce an uncontrolled element into the managerial system.
3. On the other hand, the natural resistance of the line to staff innovations probably usefully restrains over-eager efforts to apply untested procedures on a large scale.
4. Under such conditions, it is difficult to know when valuable ideas are being sacrificed.
5. The relatively weak position of staff, requiring accommodation to the line, tends to restrict their ability to engage in free, experimental innovation.

5.____

The CORRECT answer is:

A. 4, 2, 3, 1, 3   B. 1, 5, 3, 2, 4   C. 5, 3, 1, 2, 4
D. 2, 1, 4, 5, 3

KEY (CORRECT ANSWERS)

1. A
2. D
3. D
4. A
5. B

TEST 3

DIRECTIONS: Questions 1 through 4 consist of six sentences which can be arranged in a logical sequence. For each question, select the choice which places the numbered sentences in the *most logical* sequence. *PRINT THE LETTER OF THE CORRECT ANSWER IN THE SPACE AT THE RIGHT.*

1. 1. The burden of proof as to each issue is determined before trial and remains upon the same party throughout the trial.
   2. The jury is at liberty to believe one witness' testimony as against a number of contradictory witnesses.
   3. In a civil case, the party bearing the burden of proof is required to prove his contention by a fair preponderance of the evidence.
   4. However, it must be noted that a fair preponderance of evidence does not necessarily mean a greater number of witnesses.
   5. The burden of proof is the burden which rests upon one of the parties to an action to persuade the trier of the facts, generally the jury, that a proposition he asserts is true.
   6. If the evidence is equally balanced, or if it leaves the jury in such doubt as to be unable to decide the controversy either way, judgment must be given against the party upon whom the burden of proof rests.

   The CORRECT answer is:

   A. 3, 2, 5, 4, 1, 6   B. 1, 2, 6, 5, 3, 4   C. 3, 4, 5, 1, 2, 6
   D. 5, 1, 3, 6, 4, 2

   1.____

2. 1. If a parent is without assets and is unemployed, he cannot be convicted of the crime of non-support of a child.
   2. The term "sufficient ability" has been held to mean sufficient financial ability.
   3. It does not matter if his unemployment is by choice or unavoidable circumstances.
   4. If he fails to take any steps at all, he may be liable to prosecution for endangering the welfare of a child.
   5. Under the penal law, a parent is responsible for the support of his minor child only if the parent is "of sufficient ability."
   6. An indigent parent may meet his obligation by borrowing money or by seeking aid under the provisions of the Social Welfare Law.

   The CORRECT answer is:

   A. 6, 1, 5, 3, 2, 4   B. 1, 3, 5, 2, 4, 6   C. 5, 2, 1, 3, 6, 4
   D. 1, 6, 4, 5, 2, 3

   2.____

3.   1. Consider, for example, the case of a rabble rouser who urges a group of twenty   3._____
         people to go out and break the windows of a nearby factory.
     2. Therefore, the law fills the indicated gap with the crime of inciting to riot.
     3. A person is considered guilty of inciting to riot when he urges ten or more per-
         sons to engage in tumultuous and violent conduct of a kind likely to create public
         alarm.
     4. However, if he has not obtained the cooperation of at least four people, he can-
         not be charged with unlawful assembly.
     5. The charge of inciting to riot was added to the law to cover types of conduct
         which cannot be classified as either the crime of "riot" or the crime of "unlawful
         assembly."
     6. If he acquires the acquiescence of at least four of them, he is guilty of unlawful
         assembly even if the project does not materialize.
     The CORRECT answer is:

     A. 3, 5, 1, 6, 4, 2   B. 5, 1, 4, 6, 2, 3   C. 3, 4, 1, 5, 2, 6
     D. 5, 1, 4, 6, 3, 2

4.   1. If, however, the rebuttal evidence presents an issue of credibility, it is for the jury to   4._____
         determine whether the presumption has, in fact, been destroyed.
     2. Once sufficient evidence to the contrary is introduced, the presumption disap-
         pears from the trial.
     3. The effect of a presumption is to place the burden upon the adversary to come
         forward with evidence to rebut the presumption.
     4. When a presumption is overcome and ceases to exist in the case, the fact or
         facts which gave rise to the presumption still remain.
     5. Whether a presumption has been overcome is ordinarily a question for the court.
     6. Such information may furnish a basis for a logical inference.
     The CORRECT answer is:

     A. 4, 6, 2, 5, 1, 3   B. 3, 2, 5, 1, 4, 6   C. 5, 3, 6, 4, 2, 1
     D. 5, 4, 1, 2, 6, 3

KEY (CORRECT ANSWERS)

1. D
2. C
3. A
4. B

GLOSSARY OF PERSONNEL TERMS

CONTENTS

GLOSSARY OF PERSONNEL TERMS

A

Abandonment of Position—When an employee quits work without resigning. (715)

Absence Without Leave (AWOL) Absence — without prior approval, therefore without pay, that may be subject to disciplinary action. See also, *Leave Without Pay,* which is an approved absence. (630)

Administrative Workweek— A period of seven consecutive calendar days designated in advance by the head of the agency. Usually an administrative workweek coincides with a calendar week. (610)

Admonishment— Informal reproval of an employee by a supervisor; usually oral, but some agencies require written notice. (751)

Adverse Action— A removal, suspension, furlough without pay for 30 days or less, or reduction-in-grade or pay. An adverse action may be taken against an employee for disciplinary or non-disciplinary reasons. However, if the employee is covered by FPM part 752, the action must be in accordance with those procedures. Removals or reductions-in-grade based solely on unacceptable performance are covered by Part 432. Actions taken for reductions-in-force reasons are covered by Part 351. (752)

Affirmative Action — A policy followed closely by the Federal civil service that requires agencies to take positive steps to insure equal opportunity in employment, development, advancement, and treatment of all employees and applicants for employment regardless of race, color, sex, religion, national origin, or physical or mental handicap. Affirmative action also requires that specific actions be directed at the special problems and unique concerns in assuring equal employment opportunity for minorities, women and other disadvantaged groups.

Agreement—See *Collective Bargaining.*

Annuitant—A retired Federal civil service employee or a survivor (spouse or children) being paid an annuity from the Retirement Fund. (831)

Annuity—Payments to a former employee who retired, or to the surviving spouse or children. It is computed as an annual rate but paid monthly. (831)

Appeal—A request by an employee for review of an agency action by an outside agency: The right to such review-is provided by law or regulation and may include an adversary-type hearing and a written decision in which a finding of facts is made and applicable law, Executive order and regulations are applied.

Appointing Officer—A person having power by law or lawfully delegated authority to make appointments. (210, 311)

Appointment, Noncompetitive— Employment without competing with others, in the sense that it is done without regard to civil service registers, etc. Includes reinstatements, transfers, reassignments, demotions, and promotion. (335)

Appointment, Superior Qualifications—Appointment of a candidate to a position in grade 11 or above of the General Schedule at a rate above the minimum because of the candidate's superior qualifications. A rate above the minimum for the grade must be justified by the applicant's unusually high or unique qualifications, a special need of the Government for the candidate's services, or because the candidate's current pay is higher than the minimum for the grade which he or she is offered. (338, 531)

Appointment, TAPER—Abbreviation for "temporary appointment pending establishment of a register." Employment made under an OPM authority granted to an agency when there are insufficient eligibles on a register appropriate to fill the position involved. (316)

Appointment, Temporary Limited—Nonpermanent appointment of an employee hired for a specified time of one year or less, or for seasonal or intermittent positions. (316)

Appointment, Term—Nonpermanent appointment of an employee hired to work on a project expected to last over one year, but less than four years. (316)

Appropriate Unit—A group of employees which a labor organization seeks to represent for the purpose of negotiating agreements; an aggregation of employees which has a clear and identifiable community of interest and which promotes effective dealings and efficiency of operations. It may be established on a plant or installation, craft, functional or other basis. (Also known as bargaining unit, appropriate bargaining unit.) (711)

Arbitration—Final step of the negotiated grievance procedure which may be invoked by the agency or the union (not the employee) if the grievance has not been resolved. Involves use of an impartial arbitrator selected by the agency and union to render a binding award to resolve the grievance. (711)

Arbitrator—An impartial third party to whom disputing parties submit their differences for decision (award). An *ad hoc* arbitrator is one selected to act in a specific case or a limited group of cases. A permanent arbitrator is one selected to serve for the life of the agreement or a stipulated term, hearing all disputes that arise during this period. (711)

Area Office (OPM)—Forcal point for administering and implementing all OPM programs, except investigations, in the geographic area assigned. Provides personnel management advice and assistance to agencies, and personnel evaluation, recruiting and examining and special program leadership. Principal source of employment information for agencies and the public.

Audit, Work—Visit to an employee or his supervisor to verify or gather information about a position. Sometimes called "desk audit."

B

Bargaining Rights—Legally recognized right of the labor organization to represent employees in negotiations with employers. (711)

Bargaining Unit—An appropriate grouping of employees represented on an exclusive basis by a labor organization. "Appropriate" for this purpose means that it is a grouping of employees who share a community of interest and which promotes effective union and agency dealings and efficient agency operations. (711)

Basic Workweek—For a full-time employee, the 40-hour non overtime work schedule within an administrative workweek. The usual workweek consists of five 8-hour days, Monday through Friday. (610)

Break in Service—The time between separation and reemployment that may cause a loss of rights or privileges. For transfer purposes, it means not being on an agency payroll for one working day or more. For the three-year career conditional period or for reinstatement purposes, it means not being on an agency payroll for over 30 calendar days. (315)

Bumping—During reduction-in-force, the displacement of one employee by another employee in a higher group or subgroup. (351)

C

Career—Tenure of a permanent employee in the competitive service who has completed three years of substantially continuous creditable Federal service. (315)

Career-Conditional—Tenure of a permanent employee in the competitive service who *has not* completed three years of substantially continuous creditable Federal service. (315)

Career Counseling—Service available to employees to assist them in: (1) assessing their skills, abilities, interests, and aptitudes; (2) determining qualifications required for occupations within the career system and how the requirements relate to their individual capabilities; (3) defining their career goals and developing plans for reaching the goals; (4) identifying and assessing education and training opportunities and enrollment procedures; (5) identifying factors which may impair career development; and (6) learning about resources, inside or outside the agency, where additional help is available. (250)

Career Development—Systematic development designed to increase an employee's potential for advancement and career change. It may include classroom training, reading, work experience, etc. (410)

Career Ladder—A career ladder is a series of developmental positions of increasing difficulty in the same line of work, through which an employee may progress to a journeyman level on his or her personal development and performance in that series.

Career Reserved Position—A position within SES that has a specific requirement for impartiality. May be filled" only by career appointment. (920)

Ceiling, Personnel—The maximum number of employees authorized at a given time. (312)

Certification—The process by which eligibles are ranked, according to regulations, for appointment or promotion consideration. (332, 335)

Certification, Selective—Certifying only the names of eligibles who have special qualifications required to fill particular vacant positions. (332)

Certification, Top of the Register—Certifying in regular order, beginning with the eligibles at the top of the register. (332)

Change in Duty Station—A personnel action that changes an employee from one geographical location to another in the same agency. (296)

Change to Lower Grade—Downgrading a position or reducing an employee's grade. See *Demotion*. (296)

Class of Positions—All positions sufficiently similar in: (1) kind or subject matter of work; (2) level of difficulty and responsibility; and (3) qualification requirements, so as to warrant similar treatment in personnel and pay administration. For example, all Grade GS-3 Clerk-Typist positions. (511)

Classified Service—See *Competitive Service* (212)

Collective Bargaining—Performance of the mutual obligation of the employer and the exclusive (employee) representative to meet at reasonable times, to confer and negotiate in good faith, and to execute a written agreement with respect to conditions of employment, except that by any such obligation neither party shall be compelled to agree to proposals, or be required to make concessions. (Also known as collective negotiations, negotiations, and negotiation of agreement.) (711)

Collective Bargaining Agreement—A written agreement between management and a labor-organization which is usually for a definite term, and usually defines conditions of employment, and includes grievance and arbitration procedures. The terms "collective bargaining agreement" and "contract" are synonymous. (711)

Collective Bargaining Unit—A group of employees recognized as appropriate for representation by a labor organization for collective bargaining. (See *Appropriate Unit*) (711)

Compensatory Time Off—Time off (hour-for-hour) granted an employee in lieu of overtime pay. (550)

Competitive Area—For reduction-in-force, that part of an agency within which employees are in competition for retention. Generally, it is that part of an agency covered by a single appointing office. (351)

Competitive Service—Federal positions normally filled through open competitive examination (hence the term "competitive service") under civil service rules and regulations. About 86 percent of all Federal positions are in the competitive service. (212)

Competitive Status—Basic eligibility of a person to be selected to fill a position in the competitive service without open competitive examination. Competitive status may be acquired by career-conditional or career appointment through open competitive examination, or may be granted by statute, executive order, or civil service rules without competitive examination. A person with competitive status may be promoted, transferred, reassigned, reinstated, or demoted subject to the conditions prescribed by civil service rules and regulations. (212)

Consultant—An advisor to an officer or instrumentality of the Government, as distinguished from an officer or employee who carries out the agency's duties and responsibilities. (304)

Consultation—The obligation of an agency to consult the labor organization on particular personnel issues. The process of consultation lies between notification to the labor organization, which may amount simply to providing information, and negotiation, which implies agreement on the part of the labor organization. (711)

Conversion—The process of changing a person's tenure from one type of appointment to another (e.g., conversion from temporary to career-conditional). (315)

D

Demotion—A change of an employee, while serving continuously with the same agency:
(a) To a lower grade when both the old and the new positions are in the General Schedule or under the same type graded wage schedule; or
(b) To a position with a lower rate of pay when both the old and the new positions are under the same type ungraded wage schedule, or are in different pay method categories. (335, 752)

Detail—A temporary assignment of an employee to different duties or to a different position for a specified time, with the employee returning to his/her regular duties at the end of the detail. (300)

Differentials—Recruiting incentives in the form of compensation adjustments justified by: (1) extraordinarily difficult living conditions; (2) excessive physical hardship; or (3) notably unhealthful conditions. (591)

Disciplinary Action—Action taken to correct the conduct of an employee; may range from an admonishment through reprimand, suspension, reduction in grade or pay, to removal from the service. (751, 752)

Displaced Employee Program—(DEP)— A system to help find jobs for career and career-conditional employees displaced either through reduction-in-force or by an inability to accept assignment to another commuting area. (330)

Downgrading—Change of a position to a lower grade. (511, 532)

Dual Compensation—When an employee receives compensation for more than one Federal position if he/she worked more than 40 hours during the week. The term is also used in connection with compensation from a full-time Federal position as well as a retirement annuity for prior military service. (550)

Duty Station—The specific geographical area in which an employee is permanently assigned. (296)

E

Eligible—Any applicant for appointment or promotion who meets the minimum qualification requirements. (337)

Employee Development—A term which may include *career development* and *upward mobility*. It may be oriented toward development for better performance on an employee's current job, for learning a new policy or procedure, or for enhancing an employee's potential for advancement. (410, 412)

Employee, Exempt—An employee exempt from the overtime provisions of the Fair Labor Standards Act. (551)

Employee, Nonexempt—An employee subject to the overtime provision of the Fair Labor Standards Act. (551)

Employee Organization— See *Labor Organization.*

Employee Relations—The personnel function which centers upon the relationship between the supervisor and individual employees. (711)

Entrance Level Position—A position in an occupation at the beginning level grade. (511)

Environmental Differential—Additional pay authorized for a duty involving unusually severe hazards or working conditions. (532, 550)

Equal Employment Opportunity—Federal policy to provide equal employment opportunity for all; to prohibit discrimination on the grounds of age, race, color, religion, sex, national origin, or physical or mental handicap; and to promote the full realization of employees' potential through a continuing affirmative action program in each executive department and agency. (713)

Equal Employment Opportunity Commission—Regulates and enforces the Federal program for insuring equal employment opportunity, and oversees the development and implementation of Federal agencies' affirmative action programs.

Equal Pay for Substantially Equal Work—An underlying principle that provides the same pay level for work at the same level of difficulty and responsibility. (271)

Examination, Assembled—An examination which includes as one of its parts a written or performance test for which applicants are required to assemble at appointed times and places. (337)

Examination— A means of measuring, in a practical and suitable manner, qualifications of applicants for employment in specific positions. (337)

Examination, Fitness-For-Duty—An agency directed examination given by a Federal medical officer or an employee-designated, agency-approved physician to determine the employee's physical, mental, or emotional ability to perform assigned duties safely and efficiently. (339, 831)

Examination, Unassembled—An examination in which applicants are rated on their education, experience, and other qualifications as shown in the formal application and any supportive evidence that may be required, without assembling for a written or performance test. (337)

Excepted Service—Positions in the Federal civil service not subject to the appointment requirements of the competitive service. Exceptions to the normal, competitive requirements are authorized by law, executive order, or regulation. (213, 302)

Exclusive Recognition—The status conferred on a labor organization which receives a majority of votes cast in a representation election, entitling it to act for and negotiate agreements covering all employees included in an appropriate bargaining unit. The labor organization enjoying this status is known as the exclusive representative, exclusive bargaining representative, bargaining agent, or exclusive bargaining agent. (711)

Executive Inventory—An OPM computerized file which contains background information on all members of the Senior Executive Service and persons in positions at GS-16 through GS-18 or the equivalent, and individuals at lower grades who have been certified as meeting the managerial criteria for SES. It is used as an aid to agencies in executive recruiting and as a planning and management tool. (920)

Executive Resources Board—Panel of top agency executives responsible under the law for conducting the merit staffing process for career appointment to Senior Executive Service (SES) positions in the agency. Most Boards are also responsible for setting policy on and overseeing such areas as SES position planning and executive development. (920)

F

Federal Labor Relations Authority (FLRA)—Administers the Federal service labor-management relations program. It resolves questions of union representation of employees; prosecutes and adjudicates allegations of unfair labor practices; decides questions of what is or is not negotiable; and on appeal, reviews decisions of arbitrators. (5 USC 7104)

Federal Personnel Manual (FPM)—The official publication containing Federal personnel regulations and guidance. Also contains the code of Federal civil service law, selected Executive orders pertaining to Federal employment, and civil service rules. (171)

Federal Service Impasses Panel (FSIP)—Administrative body created to resolve bargaining impasses in the Federal service. The Panel may recommend procedures, including arbitration, for settling impasses, or may settle the impasse itself. Considered the legal alternative to strike in the Federal sector. (711)

Federal Wage System (FWS)—A body of laws and regulations governing the administrative processes related to trades and laboring occupations in the Federal service. (532)

Full Field Investigation—Personal investigation of an applicant's background to determine whether he/she meets fitness standards for a critical-sensitive Federal position. (736)

Function—All, or a clearly identifiable segment, of an agency's mission, including all the parts of the mission (e.g. procurement), regardless of how performed. (351)

G

General Position—A position within the Senior Executive Service that may be filled by a career, noncareer, or limited appointment. (920)

General Schedule—(GS)The graded pay system as presented by Chapter 51 of Title 5, United States Code, for classifying positions. **(511)**

Grade—All classes of positions which, although different with respect to kind or subject matter of work, are sufficiently equivalent as to (1) level of difficulty and responsibility, and (2) level of qualification requirements of the work to warrant the inclusion of such classes of positions within one range of rates of basic compensation. (511, 532)

Grade Retention—The right of a General Schedule or prevailing rate employee, when demoted for certain reasons, to retain the higher grade for most purposes for two years. (536)

Grievance, (Negotiated Procedure)—Any complaint or expressed dissatisfaction by an employee against an action by management in connection with his job, pay or other aspects of employment. Whether such complaint or expressed dissatisfaction is formally recognized and handled as a "grievance" under a negotiated procedure depends on the scope of that procedure. (711)

Grievance (Under Agency Administrative Procedure)—A request by an employee or by a group of employees acting as individuals, for personal relief in a matter of concern or dissatisfaction to the employee, subject to the control of agency management.

Grievance Procedure—A procedure, either administrative or negotiated, by which employees may seek redress of any matter subject to the control of agency management. (711, 771)

H

Handbook X-118— The official qualification standard a manual for General Schedule Positions. (338)

Handbook X-118C—The official qualification standards manual for Wage System positions. (338)

Hearing—The opportunity for contending parties under a grievance, complaint, or other remedial process, to introduce testimony and evidence and to confront and examine or cross examine witnesses. (713, 771, 772)

I

Impasse Procedures—Procedures for resolving deadlocks between agencies and union in collective bargaining. (711)

Incentive Awards—An all-inclusive term covering awards granted under Part 451 or OPM regulations. Includes an award for a suggestion submitted by an employee and adopted by management; a special achievement award for performance exceeding job requirements, or an honorary award in the form of a certificate, emblem, pin or other item. (451)

Indefinite—Tenure of a nonpermanent employee hired for an unlimited time. (316)

Injury, Work Related—For compensation under the Federal Employees' Compensation Act, a personal injury sustained while in the performance of duty. The term "injury" includes diseases proximately caused by the employment. (810)

Injury, Traumatic—Under the Federal Employees' Compensation Act, for continuation of pay purposes, a wound or other condition of the body caused by external force, including stress or strain. The injury must be identifiable by time and place of occurrence and member or function of the body affected, and be caused by a specific event or incident or series of events or incidents within a single day or work shift. (810)

Intergovernmental Personnel Assignment—Assignments of personnel to and from the Executive Branch of the Federal Government, state and local government agencies, and institutions of higher education up to two years, although a two-year extension may be permitted. The purpose is to provide technical assistance or expertise where needed for short periods of time. (334)

Intermittent—Less than full-time employment requiring irregular work hours which cannot be prescheduled. (610)

J

Job Analysis—Technical review and evaluation of a position's duties, responsibilities, and level of work and of the skills, abilities, and knowledge needed to do the work. (511, 532)

Job Enrichment—Carefully planned work assignments and/or training to use and upgrade employee skills, abilities, and interests; and to provide opportunity for growth, and encourage self-improvement. (312)

Job Freeze—A restriction on hiring and/or promotion by administrative or legislative action. (330)

Job Title— The formal name of a position as determined by official classification standards. (511, 532)

Journeyman Level—(Full Performance Level)The lowest level of a career ladder position at which an employee has learned the full range of duties in a specific occupation. All jobs below full performance level are developmental levels, through which each employee in the occupation may progress to full performance. (511)

L

Labor-Management Relations—Relationships and dealings between employee unions and management. (711)

Labor Organization—An organization composed in whole or in part of employees, in which employees participate and pay dues, and which has as a purpose dealing with an agency concerning grievances and working conditions of employment. (711)

Lead Agency—Under the Federal Wage-System, the Federal agency with the largest number of Federal wage workers in a geographical area; consequently, it has the primary role for determining wage rates for all Federal employees who work in that area and are covered by the System. (532)

Leave, Annual—Time allowed to employees for vacation and other absences for personal reasons. (630)

Leave, Court—Time allowed to employees for jury and certain types of witness service. (630)

Leave, Military—Time allowed to employees for certain types of military service. (630)

Leave, Sick—Time allowed to employees for physical incapacity, to prevent the spread of contagious diseases, or to obtain medical, dental or eye examination or treatment. (630)

Leave Without Pay (LWOP)—A temporary nonpay status and absence from duty, requested by an employee. The permissive nature of "leave without pay" distinguishes it from "absence without leave." (630)

Level of Difficulty—A classification term used to indicate the relative ranking of duties and responsibilities. (511, 532)

M

Maintenance Review—A formal, periodic review (usually annual) of all positions in an organization, or portion of an organization, to insure that classifications are correct and position descriptions are current. (511)

Major Duty—Any duty or responsibility, or group of closely related tasks, of a position which (1) determines qualification requirements for the position, (2) occupies a significant amount of the employee's time, and (3) is a regular or recurring duty. (511)

Management Official—An individual employed by an agency in a position whose duties and responsibilities require or authorize the individual to formulate, determine or influence the policies of the agency. (711)

Management Rights—The right of management to make day-today personnel decisions and to direct the work force without mandatory negotiation with the exclusive representative. (See "Reserved Rights Doctrine.") Usually a specific list of management authorities not subject to the obligation to bargain. (117)

Mediation—Procedure using a third-party to facilitate the reaching of an agreement voluntarily. (711)

Merit Promotion Program—The system under which agencies consider an employee for internal personnel actions on the basis of personal merit. (335)

Merit Systems Protection Board (MSPB)—An independent agency which monitors the administration of the Federal civil service system, prosecutes and adjudicates allegations of merit principle abuses, and hears and decides other civil service appeals. (5 USC 1205)

N

National Agency Check and Inquiry (NACI)—The Investigation of applicants for nonsensitive Federal positions by means of a name check through national investigative files and voucher inquiries. (731)

National Consultation Rights—A relationship established between the headquarters of a Federal agency and the national office of a union under criteria of the Federal Labor Relations Authority. When a union holds national consultation rights, the agency must give the union notice of proposed new substantive personnel policies, and of proposed changes in personnel policies, and an opportunity to comment on such proposals. The union has a right to: (1) suggest changes in personnel policies and have those suggestions carefully considered; (2) consult at reasonable times with appropriate officials about personnel policy matters; and (3) submit its views in writing on personnel policy matters at any time. The agency must provide the union with a written statement (which need not be detailed) of reasons for taking its final action on a policy. (711)

Negotiability—A determination as to whether a matter is within the obligation to bargain. (711)

Negotiated Grievance Procedure—A procedure applicable to members of a bargaining unit for considering grievances. Coverage and scope are negotiated by the parties to the agreement, except that the procedures may not cover certain matters designated in Title VII of the CSRA as excluded from the scope of negotiated grievance procedures. (711)

Negotiations—The bargaining process used to reach a settlement between labor and management over conditions of employment. (711)

Nominating Officer—A subordinate officer of an agency to whom authority has been delegated by the head of the agency to nominate for appointment but not actually appoint employees. (311)

O

Objection—A written statement by an agency of the reasons why it believes an eligible whose name is on a certificate is not qualified for the position to which referred. If the Examining Office sustains the objection, the agency may eliminate the person from consideration. (332)

Occupational Group—Positions of differing kinds but within the same field of work. For example, the GS-500 Accounting and Budget Occupational Group includes: General Accounting Clerical and Administrative Series; Financial Management; Internal Revenue Agent Accounting Technician; Payroll; etc. (511, 532)

Office of Personnel Management (OPM)—Regulates, administers, and evaluates the civil service program according to merit principles. (5 USC 1103)

Office of Workers Compensation Programs (OWCP)—In the Department of Labor, administers statutes that allow compensation to employees and their survivors for work-related injuries and illnesses. Decides and pays claims. (810)

Official Personnel Folder (OPF)—The official repository of employment records and documents affecting personnel actions during an employee's Federal civilian service. (293)

Overtime Work—Under Title 5, U.S. Code, officially ordered or approved work performed in excess of eight hours in a day or 40 hours in a week. Under the Fair Labor Standards Act, work in excess of 40 hours in a week by a nonexempt employee. (550, 551)

P

Pass Over—Elimination from appointment consideration of a veteran preference eligible on a certificate (candidate list), to appoint a lower ranking nonveteran, when the agency submits reasons which OPM finds sufficient. (332)

Pay Retention—The right of a General Schedule or prevailing rate employee (following a grade retention period or at other specified times when the rate of basic pay would otherwise be reduced) to continue to receive the higher rate. Pay is retained indefinitely. (536)

Pay, Severance—Money paid to employees separated by reduction-in-force and not eligible for retirement. The following formula is used, but the amount cannot be more than one year's pay:
>	*Basic Severance Pay*— *One* week's pay for each year of civilian service up to 10 years, and two weeks' pay for each year served over 10 years, plus
>	*Age Adjustment Allowance* —10 percent of the basic severance pay for each year over age 40. (550)

Performance Appraisal—The comparison, under a performance appraisal system, of an employee's actual performance against the performance standards previously established for the position. (430)

Personal Action— The process necessary to appoint, separate, reinstate, or make other changes affecting an employee (e.g., change in position assignment, tenure, etc.). (296)

Personnel Management—Management of human resources to accomplish a mission and provide individual job satisfaction. It is the line responsibility of the operating supervisor and the staff responsibility of the personnel office. (250)

Position—A specific job consisting of all the current major duties and responsibilities assigned or delegated by management. (312)

Position Change—A promotion, demotion, or reassignment. (335)

Position Classification—Analyzing and categorizing jobs by occupational group, series, class, and grade according to like duties, responsibilities, and qualification requirements. (511, 532)

Position Classifier—A specialist in job analysis who determines the titles, occupational groups, series, and grades of positions. (312)

Position Description—An official written statement of the major duties, responsibilities and supervisory relationships of a position. (312)

Position Management—The process of designing positions to combine logical and consistent duties and responsibilities into an orderly, efficient, and productive organization to accomplish agency mission. (312)

Position Survey—Agency review of positions to determine whether the positions are still needed and, if so, whether the classification and position description are correct. (312)

Position, "PL 313 Type"—Positions established under Public Law 80-313 of August 1, 1947, or similar authorities. A small group of high level professional and scientific positions generally in the competitive service, but not filled through competitive examinations. Salaries are set between GS-12 and GS-18. (534)

Preference, Compensable Disability ("CP")—Ten-point preference awarded to a veteran separated under honorable conditions from active duty, who receives compensation of 10 percent or more for a service-connected disability. Eligible "CP" veterans are placed at the top of civil service lists of eligibles for positions at GS-9 or higher. (211)

Preference, 30 Percent or More, Disabled ("CPS")—A disabled veteran whose disability is rated at 30 percent or more, entitled to special preference in appointment and during reduction in force.

Preference, Disability ("XP")—Ten-point preference in hiring for a veteran separated under honorable conditions from active duty and who has a service-connected disability or receives compensation, pension, òr disability retirement from the VA or a uniformed service. (211)

Preference, Mother ("XP")—Ten-point preference to which the mother of a deceased or disabled military veteran may be entitled. (211)

Preference, Spouse ("XP")—Ten-point preference to which a disabled military veteran's spouse may be entitled. (211)

Preference, Tentative ("TP")— Five-point veteran preference tentatively awarded an eligible who served on active duty during specified periods and was separated from military service under honorable conditions. It must be verified by the appointing officer. (211)

Preference, Veteran—The statutory right to special advantage in appointments or separations; based on a person's discharge under honorable conditions from the armed forces, for a service-connected disability. *Not* applicable to the Senior Executive Service. (211)

Preference, Widow or Widower ("XP")—Ten-point preference to which a military veteran's widow or widower may be entitled. (211)

Premium Pay—Additional pay for overtime, night, Sunday and holiday work. (550)

Prevailing Rate System—A subsystem of the Federal Wage System used to determine the employee's pay in a particular wage area. The determination requires, comparing. the_. rate of pay with the private sector for similar duties and responsibilities. (532)

Probationary Period—A trial period which is a condition of the initial competitive appointment. Provides the final indispensable test of ability, that of actual performance on the job. (315)

Promotion—A change of an employee to a higher grade when both the old and new positions are under the same job classification system and pay schedule, or to a position with higher pay in a different job classification system and pay schedule. (335)

Promotion, Career—Promotion of an employee without current competition when: (1) he/ she had earlier been competitively selected from a register or under competitive promotion procedures for an assignment intended as a matter of record to be preparation for the position being filled; or (2) the position is reconstituted at a higher grade because of additional duties and responsibilities. (335)

Promotion, Competitive—Selection of a current or former Federal civil service employee for a higher grade position, using procedures that compare the candidates on merit. (335)

Promotion Certificate—A list of best qualified candidates to be considered to fill a position under competitive promotion procedures. (335)

Q

Qualifications Review Board—A panel attached to OPM that determines whether a candidate for career appointment in the Senior Executive Service meets the managerial criteria established by law.

Qualification Requirements—Education, experience, and other prerequisites to employment or placement in a position. (338)

Quality Graduate—College graduate who was a superior student and can be hired at a higher grade than the one to which he/she would otherwise be entitled '(338)

Quality Increase—An additional within-grade increase granted to General Schedule employees for high quality performance above that ordinarily found in the type of position concerned (531).

R

Reassignment—The change of an employee, while serving continuously within the same agency, from one position to another, without promotion or demotion. (210)

Recognition—Employer acceptance of a labor organization as authorized to negotiate, usually for all members of a bargaining unit. (711) Also, used to refer to incentive awards granted under provisions of Parts 451 and 541 of OPM Regulations, and Quality Increases granted under Part 531.

Recruitment—Process of attracting a supply of qualified eligibles for employment consideration. (332)

Reduction-in-Force (RIF)—A personnel action that may be required due to lack of work or funds, changes resulting from reorganization, downward reclassification of a position, or the need to make room for an employee with reemployment or restoration rights. Involves separating an employee from his/her present position, but does not necessarily result in separation or downgrading. (351) (See also *Tenure Groups.*)

Reemployment Priority List—Career and career-conditional employees, separated by reduction-in-force, who are identified, in priority order, for reemployment to competitive positions in the agency in the commuting area where the separations occurred. (330)

Reemployment Rights—Right of an employee to return to an agency after detail, transfer, or appointment to: (1) another Executive agency during an emergency; (2) an international organization; or (3) other statutorily covered employment, e.g., the Peace Corps. (352)

Register—A list of eligible applicants compiled in the order of their relative standing for referral to Federal jobs, after competitive civil service examination. (332,210)

Reinstatement— Noncompetitive reemployment in the competitive service based on previous service under a career or career-conditional appointment. (315)

Removal—Separation of an employee for cause or because of continual unacceptable performance. (432, 752)

Representation—Actions and rights of the labor organization to consult and negotiate with management on behalf of the bargaining unit and represent employees in the unit. (711)

Representation Election—Election conducted to determine whether the employees in an appropriate unit (See *Bargaining Unit)* desire a labor organization to act as their exclusive representative. (711)

Reprimand—An official rebuke of an employee. Normally in writing and placed in the   temporary side of an employee's OPF-(751)

"Reserved Rights Doctrine"—Specific functions delegated to management by Title VII of CSRA that protect management's ability to perform its necessary functions and duties. (See Management Rights.) Delegates to management specific functions not subject to negotiation except as to procedures and impact. (711)

Resignation—A separation, prior to retirement, in response to an employee's request for the action. It is a voluntary expression of the employee's desire to leave the organization and must not be demanded as an alternative to some other action to be taken or withheld. (715)

Restoration Rights—Employees who enter military service or sustain a compensable job-related injury or disability are entitled to be restored to the same or higher employment status held prior to their absence. (353)

Retention Preference—The relative standing of employees competing in a reduction-inforce. Their standing is determined by veteran's preference, tenure group, length of service, and performance appraisal. (351)

Retention Register—A list of all employees, arranged by competitive level, describing their retention preference during reductions-in-force. (351)

Retirement—Payment of an annuity after separation from a position under the Civil Service Retirement System and based on meeting age and length of service requirements. The types of retirement are:

> *Deferred* - An employee with five years civilian service who separates or transfers to a position not under the Retirement Act, may receive an annuity, does not withdraw from the Retirement Fund. (.83:1)
>
> *Disability* - An immediate annuity paid to an employee under the retirement system who has completed five years of civilian service and has suffered a mental, emotional, or physical disability not the result of the employee's vicious habits, intemperance, or willful misconduct, (831)
>
> *Discontinued Service* - An immediate annuity paid to an employee who is involuntarily separated, through no personal fault of the employee, after age 50 and 20 years of service, or at any age with 25 years of service. This annuity is reduced by 1/6 of one percent for each full month under age 55 (two percent per year). (831)
>
> *Optional* - The minimum combinations of age and service for this kind of immediate annuity are: age 62 with five years of service; age 60 with 20 years of service; age 55 with 30 years of service. (831)

Review, Classification—An official written request for reclassification of a position. Previously called a classification appeal.

S

Schedules A, B, and C—Categories of positions excepted from the competitive service by regulation. (213)

>*Schedule A*—Positions other than confidential or policy determining, for which it is not practical to examine.
>*Schedule B*— Positions other than confidential or policy determining for which it is not practical to hold a competitive examination.
>*Schedule C*—Positions of a confidential or policy determining character.

Senior Executive Service—A separate personnel system for persons who set policy and administer programs at the top levels of the Government (equivalent to GS-16 through Executive Level IV). (920)

Service Computation Date-Leave—The date, either actual or adjusted, from which service credit is accumulated for determining the rate of leave accrual; it may be different from the service computation date, which determines relative standing in a subgroup for reduction-in-force, or service computation date for retirement. (296)

Service Record Card (Standard Form 7)—A brief of the employee's service history. It is kept on file in accordance with agency disposition instructions. (295)

Special Salary Rates—Salary rates higher than regular statutory schedule; established for occupations in which private enterprise pays substantially more than the regular Federal Schedule. (530)

Spoils System—The personnel system characterized by the political appointment and removal of employees without regard to merit. (212)

Staffing—Use of available and projected personnel through recruitment, appointment, reassignment, promotion, reduction-in-force, etc., to provide the work force required to fulfill the agency's mission. (250)

Standard Form—171 ("Personal Qualification Statement") Used in applying for a Federal position through a competitive examination. (295)

Standards of Conduct For Labor Organization—In the Federal sector, a code governing internal democratic practices and fiscal responsibility, and procedures to which a labor organization must adhere to be eligible to receive any recognition. (711)

Steward (Union Steward)—A local union's representative in a plant or department, appointed by the union to carry out union duties, adjust grievances, collect dues and solicit new members. Stewards are employees trained by the union to carry out their duties.

Strike—Temporary stoppage of work by a group of employees to express a grievance, enforce a demand for changes in conditions of employment, obtain recognition, or resolve a dispute with management. *Wildcat strike*- a strike not sanctioned by union and which may violate a collective agreement. *Quickie strike*- a spontaneous or unannounced strike of short duration. *Slowdown-a* deliberate reduction of output without an actual strike in order to force concessions from *an* employer. *Walkout* -same as strike. Strikes are illegal for Federal employees. (711)

Suitability—An applicant's or employee's fitness for Federal employment as indicated by character and conduct. (731)

Supervisor—An individual employed by an agency having authority, in the interest of the agency, to hire, direct, assign, promote, reward, transfer, furlough, lay off, recall, suspend, discipline-or remove employees, to adjust their grievances, or to effectively recommend such action-if the exercise of the authority is not merely routine or clerical in nature but requires the consistent exercise of independent judgment. With respect to any unit which includes firefighters or nurses, the term "supervisor" includes only those individuals who devote a preponderance of their employment time to exercising such authority. (711).

Survey, Classification—An intensive study of all positions in an organization or organizational segment to insure their correct classification.

Suspension—Placing an employee, for disciplinary reasons, in a temporary status without duties and pay. (751, 752)

T

Tenure—The time an employee may reasonably expect to serve under a current appointment. It is governed by the type of appointment, without regard to whether the employee has competitive status. (210)

Tenure Groups—Categories of employees ranked in priority order for retention during reduction in force . Within each group, veterans are ranked above nonveterans. For the competitive service, the tenure groups are, in descending order:
Group I—Employees under career appointments and not serving probation.
Group II—Employees serving probation, career-conditional employees, and career employees in obligated positions.
Group III—Employees with indefinite appointments, status quo employees under any other nonstatus, nontemporary appointment. (351)
For the *excepted service,* they are in descending order:
Group I—Permanent employees, not serving a trial period, whose appointments carry no restriction or condition, such as "indefinite" or "time-limited".
Group II—Employees serving trial periods, those whose tenure is indefinite because they occupy obligated positions, and those whose tenure is equivalent to career-conditional in the competitive service.
Group III—Employees whose tenure is indefinite, but not potentially permanent, and temporary employees who have completed one year of current continuous employment. (351)

Tenure Subgroups—The ranking of veterans above nonveterans in each tenure group, as follows:

Subgroup AD—Veterans with service-connected disability of 30% or more.
Subgroup A— All other veterans
Subgroup B—Nonveterans

Time-in-Grade Restriction—A requirement intended to prevent excessively rapid promotions in the General Schedule. Generally, an employee may not be promoted more than two grades within one year to positions up to GS-5. At GS-5 and above, an employee must serve a minimum of one year in grade, and cannot be promoted more than one grade, or two grades if that is the normal progression. (300)

Tour of Duty—The hours of a day (a daily tour of duty) and the day of an administrative workweek (weekly tour of duty) scheduled in advance and during which an employee is required to work regularly. (610)

Training—Formal instruction or controlled and planned exposure to learning. (410)

Transfer—A change of an employee, without a break in service of one full workday, from a position in one agency to a position in another agency. (315)

Transfer of Function—For reduction-in-force, the transfer of a continuing function from one agency or competitive area to another, or when the competitive area in which work is performed is moved to another commuting area. (315)

U

Unemployment Compensation—Income maintenance payments to former Federal employees who: (1) are unemployed; (2) file a claim at a local employment office for unemployment compensation; and (3) register for work assignment. The program is administered through state and D.C. employment service offices, which determine eligibility and make the payments. (850)

Unfair Labor Practices—Prohibited actions by agency management and labor organizations. (711)

Union—See *Labor Organization.*

Upward Mobility—Systematic career development requiring competitive selection in positions that provide experience and training leading to future assignments in other, more responsible positions.(410)

V

Veteran—A person entitled to preference under 5 USC 2108, including a spouse, widow, widower, or mother entitled to preference under the law. (211)

Voucher—In staffing terms, a formal inquiry to employers, references, professors, and others who presumably know a job applicant well enough to describe job qualifications and personal character. (337)

W

Wage Employees—Those employees-in trades, crafts, or labor occupations covered by the Federal Wage System, whose pay is fixed and adjusted periodically in accordance with prevailing rates. (532)

Within-Grade Increase—A salary increase provided in certain Government pay plans based upon time-in-grade and acceptable or satisfactory work performance. Also known as "periodic increase" or "step increase." (531)

NOTE:

Numbers in parentheses after the definitions refer to the appropriate FEDERAL PERSONNEL MANUAL (FPM) Chapter indicated.